T0195596

TIME/SAND MEMoirs:
Healing of My Fractured Soul

CELESTE NEWHOME

BALBOA.PRESS
A DIVISION OF HAY HOUSE

Balboa Press books may be ordered through booksellers or by contacting:

Balboa Press
A Division of Hay House
1663 Liberty Drive
Bloomington, IN 47403
www.balboapress.com
844-682-1282

Because of the dynamic nature of the Internet, any web addresses or links contained in this book may have changed since publication and may no longer be valid. The views expressed in this work are solely those of the author and do not necessarily reflect the views of the publisher, and the publisher hereby disclaims any responsibility for them.

The author of this book does not dispense medical advice or prescribe the use of any technique as a form of treatment for physical, emotional, or medical problems without the advice of a physician, either directly or indirectly. The intent of the author is only to offer information of a general nature to help you in your quest for emotional and spiritual well-being. In the event you use any of the information in this book for yourself, which is your constitutional right, the author and the publisher assume no responsibility for your actions.

Any people depicted in stock imagery provided by Getty Images are models, and such images are being used for illustrative purposes only. Certain stock imagery © Getty Images.

Scripture quotations marked KJV are from the Holy Bible, King James Version (Authorized Version). First published in 1611. Quoted from the KJV Classic Reference Bible, Copyright © 1983 by The Zondervan Corporation.

Print information available on the last page.

ISBN: 978-1-9822-7221-0 (sc)
ISBN: 978-1-9822-7222-7 (e)

Library of Congress Control Number: 2021915091

Balboa Press rev. date: 07/24/2021

Contents

Acknowledgments

As I wrote *Time/Sand Memoirs: Healing of My Fractured Soul*, like a movie, the reel spun inside my head, and I saw the faces and felt the compassion of those who unknowingly changed my path and the moments and years of the strong and gentle souls who influenced my journey. How blessed I have been that we met during this lifetime.

There have been many lessons for me to learn in this incarnation, some wondrous and others crippling. As I saw myself grow, I saw the phoenix rising from the ashes, I found strength and discernment, and I now resonate with the offerings of many lifetimes to find myself here.

This acknowledgement is to let you know that I remember.

There are always those friends who are present and who make life so much easier—the cornerstones of the foundation that is being built; the treasures that have no idea of the role they play or played in my life; the gems that adorned my pathway.

They are ones who were there no matter what was happening, who took me to the hospital, to emergency rooms, to dinner; who sat with me and took care of me when I was sick, helped me clean my house, remodeled my house, helped me with projects, visited on holidays so I wasn't alone, invited me into his home when I needed shelter for various reasons, took care of my guinea pig as I traveled, helped me move, helped me get settled. Helped me, helped me, helped me. Although it was never one-sided, I deeply honor one special friend who liked me just for being me, no matter what.

Then there was the friend who got together with me every weekend and had amazing adventures. Movies, dinner, out-of-town shopping trips, holidays, traveling overseas, traveling in the United States, and the out-of-town dancing excursions. She would add that fun flare and take videos of us as I drove down the road, singing and playing. We laughed so much all the time; it was such a treasure to be together. And we cried together and felt each other's pain as life took its turns; we helped each other to hang on. If I was climbing a mountain in my life, she would go ahead to scope things out, or if it was her, I would go ahead and feel the energy of what was to come. It was a wonderfully balanced friendship.

And the friend who guided me on my spiritual journey for so many years with encouragement and love; who helped when medical issues arose and kept my chakras balanced as I continued my growth in light; who listened to my heartaches, even as they sounded like a broken record to me at times, helping me to keep moving forward. She was always on my professional team in some capacity, offering love and ideas. At times, she was in the role of not only friend but teacher and "mother." A beautiful spirit. The night she told me I needed to find a psychic to help me understand my gifts, I felt an abandonment. In reality, the butterfly was unfolding from its cocoon, and I was given my wings to fly.

To each person in my life who offered their love in time of need, to those who saw the light I carried within when I couldn't, thank you. Each one of you has a space in my heart and in my growth.

Finally, last but certainly not least, to my publication and editorial team, who spent much time on the phone helping me sort through my manuscript. For the hours spent reading and editing this memoir, thank you all so very much for your wonderful gifts and talents in making this a reality for me and for those who gain momentum to change their own stars. Anything is possible!

Introduction

Sands of Time
As passion fills the heart,
So does hope expand
A river flowing is not always smooth,
But navigates with desire,
So too do the Sands of Time.

Time/Sand Memoirs: Healing of My Fractured Soul is my account of my challenging yet healing journey through life. It is a compilation of my struggle, abuse, illness, family, marriage, relationships, hope, love, spirituality, and resilience; an unfolding of life in my earliest years and continuing into the present, depicting my pathway to the point of this publication.

My education includes a master's degree in social work; I'm a licensed independent clinical social worker and a licensed alcohol and drug counselor. My undergraduate degrees include a bachelor's degree in social work, an associate of arts degree, an associate in applied sciences degree, and certification as a human care specialist. I also have distinctions in two National Honor Societies, Phi Theta Kappa, Eta Zeta (the national honor society of community and junior colleges) and Alpha Delta Mu, Gamma Nu (the national honor society of social workers). All of this has allowed me a lifelong career in psychotherapy and as an addictions specialist. I have done extensive research on the correlation between childhood abuse, mental illness, and chemical dependency. Science and psychology has determined that disease and substance abuse is a direct indicator of childhood abuse (Mayo Clinic offers a wealth of information on the study of this subject).

My studies in the esoteric, metaphysical, and psychic world of prophetic gifts have earned certifications as an advanced psychic and a tarot reader. I practice energy healing, and I am certified as Level II with Healing Beyond Borders, Healing Touch.

As I begin this memoir, I invite the reader to join me on a raw and mystical path that connects to the heart space. The curiosity to open doors to spirituality—to the possibility of life, every thought, and every action being interconnected to quantum reality, allowing one to imagine what life is like in a world to which only few are connected—is presented in a magical flow from hardship to new beginnings.

My autobiographical snapshot of early life begins by describing the harshness of abuse, abandonment, and rejection by a narcissistic mother with untreated alcoholism toward her daughter, the horrors of witnessed abuse by an alcoholic father and stepfather, rejection from my alcoholic father, the fear I harbored that carried into adulthood and later years, and how I was affected by the illness of those who cared for me.

I will share some of the horror stories of what I witnessed between my parents in this account, for sharing the past brings healing in the present. The memories are like stories in the picture book of my mind, deep sorrow, and devastation.

I share compassionately a ten-year span of illness, in which I explain the relentless dark ball of energy, a rather esoteric and intuitive sense of how my body experienced illness through meditation and prophetic gifts of clairvoyance, clairsentience, and claircognizance that moved around in my body and what occurred in each organ as a result of this dark ball of energy.

The section also shows my resiliency as I learned to gain power in my life, how it changed my path through spiritual beliefs, and how I was able to disengage with the dark ball of energy to focus on health and assume wellness. I speak of the "dark ball of energy"; this is how spirit revealed this congestive energy to me in meditation. The areas affected were literally *dark balls of energy*, and I saw and felt them move about my body.

I will share a revealing collection of vignettes from my life, which may well be viewed as tragedy or negativity, that shifted into loving and positive narratives that instilled hope and the experience of unconditional love to prevail. From a child who knew only rejection and abandonment grew a woman of confidence with the ability to give and receive what was so freely given to her.

Prophetic gifts are the foundation of this memoir, and I describe a lifetime of unfolding events and journeys that my guides channeled to me from the spirit world. Each person has a spirit guide (or guides) who accompanies them throughout life to aid in their journeys. Meditation and divine connection with your inner self is an inspirational pathway to connect with your guides.

Many books on spirituality speak of guides, ascended masters, divine goddesses, archangels, guardian angels, and helpers from the spirit world. We are never alone, and help is always a breath away. I mention one example for gaining knowledge on this subject (Doreen Virtue, *Archangels & Ascended Master: A Guide to Working with Divinities and Deities*).

I then return to the mystical journey of spirituality that I have traveled, with a chronological account of my earliest recollection in realizing my prophetic gifts and the unfolding of them in my life. As I lay the foundation of my spirituality, I open more to the inner knowing of my soul and the path I will travel.

In the final section of this memoir, I lend knowledge to the teachings and awareness that have unfolded in my spiritual awakening, offering hope to the reader that all things are possible. The inner reconciliation of oneself with the present is the journey of the soul.

Throughout the book, I have woven poetry and prose that I have written, allowing the reader to follow yet another journey—the journey through the eye of an awakened spirit, the feelings that were the foundation of each section, and a magical summary to give imagination to the reader of the feelings that were generated from memories. The reader also has the opportunity to view each quote as a collective that tells a story and each poem as a collective that speaks yet another story. This mystical journey of the memoir displays its ability to be layered and to reveal three stories, one through quotes starting at the beginning, one through poems that begin their journey in this introduction, and one, most notably, the memoir itself.

The afterword shares a last story of illness unrelated to the dark ball of energy but nonetheless, it includes a wonderful healing. Over a hundred healers from different areas in the world sent remote healing to me. I was so elevated from the energy that it was as if my feet did not touch the ground. My attitude was one of complete positivity, and I knew I would be healed—and thus, I was. At the conclusion of this memoir, I had two follow-up checks with my urologist, and I continue to be cancer-free eight months later!

I complete this memoir with a portion of a song I wrote during the 2020 pandemic, the riots stemming from structural and systemic racial injustice, and the discourse of society, in an attempt to stand strong and grasp reality as it slowly oozes from beneath their feet. The song, "The Freedom Fighter/the Lover," is dedicated to all who have fought, who will fight, and who will heal from the tragedies of abuse in all forms.

Go within. Meditate. Journal. Write stories, poems, and thoughts. Take classes. Attend spiritual conferences. Talk to each other. Allow love as it unfolds. Learn boundaries. See therapists. Participate in healing groups and ceremonies. Look in the mirror and learn to say, "I love you, I accept you, I cherish you, and I am you!" Connect with your inner child, your spirit child, who has been with you for all of eternity. This little one has carried the burdens. Love this child, for it is you.

Now enter the etheric world of spirit and the journey of a woman who shifts from *survivor* to *liver of life* as the journey unfolds.

1

Reflection

The Light has never been dim
It was only the thickness of the patch over my eye

As thoughts rush in like a mighty wave, welling up with impending approach, they share their secret knowledge. I allow the ebb and flow to occur. What I find lying on the beach are the shells of you, and I see me. As I pick up each sandy shell, I see what is written. I feel the compulsion to pen words on paper that would at least feebly seek to find feeling in another—as an anchor for his or her own soul.

What is written in this book are the memoirs of a child and adult. It is my hope that in reading this memoir, you may find your own hope and inspiration, to see a door opening, to gain strength in order to move forward in life. May the words in this memoir also be a turning point, a guide to the future, for it is in accepting the present and releasing the past that a future is born. I offer a recollection of childhood memories as I grew to adulthood to aid the reader in understanding the path my life has taken in order to connect with the healing of my fractured soul. The memoir weaves prose and poetry, divinely inspired throughout, for yet a more mystical connection to this story.

The following chapter, titled "An Unassimilated View of My Life," is my way of assimilating others or, more specifically, the culture of alcoholism into a society that continues to shamefully hide, without allowance, the integration of addiction into the wider scope of society.

And as we will come to see, our journeys are long and sometimes tedious, sometimes joyful; other times, we want them to end quickly, and yet other times, linger forever. The unlimited mind has its own imprint upon our souls, and one thing I know for certain:

feelings are what remain, long after the thought has gone into a refuge of its own. It's the feeling that has found its bed in time.

My thoughts now find their own paths, uncovering what has been covered. The heart does not forget, for the heart remembers throughout eternity and continues its journey to the center of what love is, the one of what is. Imagine your heart—*your* heart—in all of its beautifully pumping enthusiasm, for just one day. Imagine the emotion of a thousand lifetimes traveling through your heart and the great connection it has to all that is, all that was, beating in that small area of your chest and the memories it holds, the incredible knowledge it has, and how much time you spend each day, trying to convince it now to not have the feelings, the pain, the memories, only allowing it to feel what you think it should feel. Separating from the truth of who we are has injured our souls.

I sometimes see the angels weeping because they know the truth about who we are when we do not. Lifetimes have added layers to what we see about the truth, within and without. I believe the angels applaud when we feel even a spark of who we are.

I see heaven as divine light with infinite cords, like a vast network of interconnectedness, linking each of us to one another, like tiny lamps lit, as if we gaze into a star-filled night, and each light is one of us.

Late one summer's evening, I was lying in an open grassy area of what I deemed to be a magical forest. It was very quiet, with only the sound of crickets and tree frogs singing their evening songs. The tall spruce trees surrounding the edge of the grassy area where I lay resembled great forest guards, protecting all that lived within. Occasionally, the silence was broken by the sound of twigs or a branch that snapped for a brief moment. I imagined fairies and gnomes busily scurrying with their tiny lanterns as I saw lightning bugs dancing among the trees and the tall prairie grass on either side of me.

As I lay in a peaceful pool of fantasy, taken in by the magic of the darkness, I looked up and began to view the vastness of the universe, with a million stars that were twinkling only for me at that very moment. I thought about the stillness of my surroundings and the amazing grace that had created all of this and how I, as one small speck, could see what I was seeing. The peace that calmed my senses from the silence was so overwhelming that it was difficult for me to do anything but shut down my thoughts for the time and appreciate this wonderment, the freeing, in a way I had so longed to do. I then realized the separateness I experienced from my human body and the desire to become one with what is.

Perhaps that is why, as spiritual beings in human bodies, we long to find closeness with others and, yet more importantly, with one divine-source energy—God, the one we feel love from and toward.

In my life, there have been many journeys, all of which have brought me to where I am today. As I continue to travel this pathway of enlightenment, I have chosen—or perhaps unknowingly, I have been chosen—to be blessed with many teachers. Life is a lesson and, as I have come to learn, earth school is one of the most challenging. We experience the five senses—touch, taste, sight, hearing, and smell—yet most often, we find them to be an expectation rather than a gift.

A sixth sense we are capable of is extrasensory perception (ESP), and at this time, ESP appears to be the least talked-about sense, with certain myths attached to it. Our bodies are surrounded by electromagnetic fields that interact with other electromagnetic fields. These are known as frequencies or vibrations and are unseen by the human eye. Quantum physics identifies these forces as being the life force of all that makes up our universe.

ESP adheres to electromagnetic fields; conscious interactions allow the ability to see, feel, hear, sense, smell, and taste others, whether they are alive or deceased. I believe this sense is much more prominent than is recognized, with many communicating in an unconscious state, thus allowing intuition, which is the knowing that speaks to us, guiding our pathways, if recognized, and in tune with our still small voice within.

Two friends and I are able to connect frequently through mental telepathy. I also can feel their different energies when one or the other connects. We have been sending messages to each other for the past three or more years. One evening, as I sat in my meditation room after coming out of a deep connection with divine-source energy, I received a text message that read, "I know that you know that I am thinking about you." I just wrote back, "Yes."

The other person spent three hours with me one evening, and we spoke only a few words verbally; the conversation we had was through mental telepathy. At the end of the evening, I said, "We did not talk much," and laughed.

He said, "Oh, but we said volumes to each other!"

This energetic connection happens daily between one of them and me.

The prophetic gifts I experience allow me clairvoyance (clear seeing; seeing images), clairsentience (clear feeling; sensing other people's emotions), and claircognizance (clear knowing; recognizing when something is going to happen). I am also able, at times, to communicate with those who are deceased, and I have the wonderful gift of healing touch, which I continue to explore. It has been an exceptional journey for me to have amazingly insightful teachers in my life who have helped me to develop these incredible gifts.

A great awakening is happening on our planet at this time, and many souls are coming back to experience the shift from the third-dimensional frame of reference to the fifth dimension. Our divine Creator, source energy, Father/Mother God has orchestrated this complete spiritual, emotional, and physical shift to bring to fruition the consciousness of unconditional love.

The Heartbeat of Time

What is time but imagination,
Floating through space on an energetic wave.
The only confinement is what it demands,
   A box of hours, a circadian cycle, a Gregorian map.
   Once passed, only memories remain of what was.
   Perhaps only the development of consciousness or the aging of the body allows some sort of context to envelope an embodiment of existence,
   To gain an attempt of nonsensical thoughts, feelings, behaviors that only erode within the confines of time.
   There's only one constant continuum, with sounds of the second hand as it makes its rotation—tick, tock, lub, dub—the beat of the heart, dancing to the cosmic rhythm, endless, allowing, giving, receiving the life force of all that is.
   And it is only in allowing that the heartbeat of the universe, with the soul of the universe beating its song of love, lasts for eternity. For it is the soul that remembers after death, love that is, that was, that remains.

2

An Unassimilated View of My Life

Peeking out from under the blanket,
which she hid unknowingly,
was yet another window to look through,
one that was free of fear

When I was six months old, my mother gave care of me to my maternal grandmother and grandfather. My mother worked nights, and my father, who was an active alcoholic, spent his free time out drinking and, at times, womanizing. My mother made her choice not to parent before I was born, after assigning my brother's care to his father.

Periodically, my mother would have me live with her briefly, at which time I would witness the horrific abuse she encountered. She retaliated against me, and then it was back to my grandparents' home.

What I've written in this book are the memoirs of a child and adult. I was a beautiful child with long, golden hair and bright green eyes, a child born into an alcoholic family, whose caregivers were alcoholic, with the exception of my maternal grandmother and my brother. My mother gave my brother, Michael, to his father when he was seven years old, a year before I was born, due to her inability to protect and care for him. She told me one day, "Michael used to sit on the couch and shake whenever your dad would enter the room; he was so afraid of him."

The only thing I could think of was, *What about me, Mom? Why did you subject me to horror?*

My mother, father, stepfathers (of which there were two), and other family members all had the disease of alcoholism. My mother also experienced a character disorder that I identified in the DSM-V (*Diagnostic & Statistical Manual of Mental Disorders*) as a narcissistic personality disorder. This led her to four marriages and divorces. My father and stepfather, who followed the divorce of my parents, were brutally abusive to my mother, and, as stated previously, I witnessed this behavior until later in my teenage years. In return, she was abusive to me, verbally, emotionally, and physically.

Both of my parents lived an incredibly tumultuous life with alcohol and made very poor decisions because of it. They had no parenting skills, and parenting was not what they wanted for their lives. I believe, however, that my brother, who was my half brother from my mother's previous marriage, and I were the winners. He no longer had to live in fear of his life, and I did only on occasion, which led to witnessing devastating abuse and suffering post-traumatic stress symptoms for most of my life. I never knew if my father was going to kill us when he was drunk; he threatened to do so many times. I spent a significant amount of time hiding when I was a child because I lived in fear whenever I was with my mother.

Living with my grandparents still involved alcohol, although on a less frequent basis. My grandfather was an alcoholic whose addiction came to life on weekends, a binge drinker when he was not working. He was a gruff man, tall, thin, and balding. When he spoke, it was usually in commands or orders. He had an adverse reaction to dishes sitting in the sink and not being washed immediately after use. It was a common thread among family members, how he reacted to dishes left sitting in the sink.

Daily, we could hear him bellow, "Get out there and get those dishes done!"

Then Grandma would whisper, "I'll wash them and you wipe; then he won't say anything anymore." So, seldom to never did you ever see a dirty dish in my grandparents' home.

Another of my grandfather's issues was when my grandmother would do mending for others. He always grumbled about it, and nine out of ten times, he would walk into her bedroom where the sewing machine sat and say in his gruff voice, "As long as you're sitting there, I have a button that needs to be sewn on my shirt."

After he had turned and walked away, Grandma would raise her arms up in the air, look at me, as I was fascinated by her ability to create as she sewed, and say with a smirk,

"I knew he'd be in here. I think he rips those buttons off his shirts just so I can stop what I'm doing and do this for him."

It's like a tape recording in my mind, the ritualistic happenings in this house where I lived with my grandparents.

When my grandfather would drink, he would go down to the basement, where he hid his bottle of liquor. When he came up from the basement, he was a different man. He was calmer, smiled, and actually said nice things to us. He thought we never knew about his hidden bottles of liquor, but everyone knew about them.

Grandma, on the other hand, was a very short woman, somewhat rotund, even-tempered (unless my grandfather got too overbearing), and loved to laugh, dance, and have fun. She found solace in fishing; that was her form of meditation. She would sit by the lake almost every day by herself and fish. She enjoyed the quietness, which took her away from being on guard around my grandfather's expectations of perfection. My grandfather's expectations were for her to iron even the bed sheets and his boxer shorts—not a tradition that I wanted to carry on.

When I was a little girl, Grandma would turn on the kitchen radio and say, "Come on, Celeste." I'd get so excited, and she'd take my hands in hers, and we'd dance around the kitchen. It was such fun; we'd laugh and all would be right in our little world at that time.

But as life was in those days, a constant barrage of drunk people and card playing filled the home where I was raised on most weekends. Loud, sometimes angry drunken people who smoked so many cigarettes that the rooms would be blue from the heavy toxicity of the smoke. My grandmother did not drink or smoke but participated in card playing because that was what life was about at that time. If I ever needed anything, though, she would stop playing cards and take care of me, even if my mother was present, because my mother would be just as drunk as everyone else.

As my life began to unfold at a very young age, I could never understand the anger and contempt that people had for each other. It never made sense to me how someone could say "I love you" and the next moment say the most heart-wrenching words that pierced the soul like a dagger.

As a young child, I would see my father kiss my mother and show love and consideration toward her, and the next day, I'd witness him maliciously beating her. I watched him bang her head over and over against a corner of the kitchen cupboard one afternoon at my paternal grandparents' home. I was crying and begging and yelling, "Stop, Daddy! Stop hurting Mommy!" As I watched her screaming and trying to get away, he kept pounding her head as he held it in place, with his hands over each of her ears, banging it against the pointed corner of the cupboard. I was a little four-year-old girl, and I was terrified and sobbing. I thought he was going to kill my mother! My father's mother and my maternal aunt were present, but no one could stop this. They were yelling at my father, "Don! Stop, stop, stop it!" My aunt grabbed my arm, and she ran out the door, dragging me behind her to the neighbor's house. She yelled, "I have to call the police!" My paternal grandparents would not let my aunt use the phone at their house. The rest of it is a blank to me.

Much of my time, when I stayed with my mother, was spent running across the street and hiding on the front porch of a neighbor's house. My parents lived in an apartment above a business on the east side of town; my mother worked, and my father spent most of his time drinking. He would come home late at night and start his drunken rampages. My mother would then scream, "Hurry, Celeste, run, run!" And I would run as fast as my little legs would allow. My mother would have my arm, pulling me across the street. She would pound on the neighbor's door and fearfully cry, "Please let me use the phone again. He is drunk and destroying the apartment."

Soon, the police would come, and I could hear my father arguing with them as I hid. They would adamantly tell him, "Mr. Newhome, you have to go somewhere else for the night. You are drunk and can't stay here." He was never arrested.

Periodically, my mother would come to my grandparents' home for a few nights to sleep. She was afraid of my father, and if he was out drinking, she would stay away from him if she could—although I do remember many a night when he would pound on my grandparents' door, yelling, "Mary, Mary! Get your ass out here right now!"

I would lie in my grandmother's bed, shaking; I was so frightened.

My grandma would say, "Just be real quiet; maybe he will go away."

Of course, he seldom left. Sometimes, the police would come, and other times, my grandmother would get him to leave.

I was four years old when I started school. I was very young and timid. I was also given my first bicycle with training wheels on it. I had a five-year-old friend who lived down the street from me. He and I became inseparable when I stayed with my parents. It is remarkable to me that I remember this little boy so well. We would sit and talk to each other; he knew his little friend lived in a dangerous home with alcoholic parents. He was the only friend I had at the time, and he was very kind to me. God always provided someone to help, and when I was four years old, it was this little boy.

One evening, my mother and I were watching television, and my father stumbled in the door, drunk and angry. He grabbed my mother and pushed her to the floor. He kicked her in the stomach and then reached down and grabbed her by the shoulders, lifted her off the floor, and slapped her. She fell to the floor again. I cried and screamed, "Mommy, Mommy!"

My mother managed to crawl away from him and reached for my hand. His back was turned, and she used all of her strength to get up. We ran as fast as we could out the door and down the street. He was right behind us, yelling, "I'm going to kill you when I get my hands on you!" We just kept running. He got closer, and I thought this was the end. My mom and I ran up to a house and burst through the front door. The people who lived in the house came running, and my mother said, "My husband is out there and wants to kill us. Please help us!"

I don't know what happened after that. My young mind was a blur.

When I was with my mother, I was never safe. She did not know how to keep me safe, and she did not know how to keep herself safe. I was endangered almost every day that I was with her.

I remember the morning when the police came knocking on our door and told my mother there had been an accident. They had found my father's car, but they hadn't found him. My mother and I drove to the scene of the accident. Across from a large park in my hometown, there was a little bar that had a house attached to it. As we drove up, I said, "Mommy, there's Daddy's car!"

She was speechless. He had driven his car right through the front of the house, and it was partially stuck inside of the house. My mother spoke with the police, and a wrecker was called to pull the car out of the house. Again, I do not know what happened after this incident. Sometimes, I think it was more than my young mind could grasp.

There was just so much trauma all the time. The only reprieve I had was when I was with my grandparents. And even though my grandfather was a weekend alcoholic, he was not abusive and usually went uptown to drink. He eventually would come home and pass out, unless there was a card party at the house. These parties were more frequent when I was quite young.

My mother had been staying at my grandparents' home again for a few days and decided to take me home with her once more. When we arrived at my parents' home, I could feel something was not right. My mother entered first, and I followed her. Objects had been thrown around in the living room, and when we walked into the bedroom, I couldn't believe my little eyes. I started crying, "Mommy, let's go, let's go!" I was panicking.

There on the bed were all of my mother's clothes, torn to shreds. The heels were all broken off her high-heeled shoes. My parent's wedding picture lay on the top of the heap—the glass from the frame was broken and perfume was poured all over it.

My mother said, "Oh, my God," and started crying.

I wanted to run away but didn't know where to go or what to do. I was so afraid he would come back again. I was afraid we would be killed. I begged my mother to leave. "Please, Mommy, let's go. Please, let's go." I could hear my voice, but she paid no attention to me. Again, I do not know what happened from that point on. My five-year-old mind could not handle the overload of trauma, and I seemed to have blacked out.

I would like to add that I was born in 1950, and in the early 1950s, men were not arrested for beating their wives or children. It took several more years—not until 1994—before domestic violence became a crime. The abuse I witnessed and experienced from my parents' behavior up to that point all occurred before I was seven years old.

The repercussions of the types of behaviors that I witnessed haunt my thoughts at certain times, which always opens the door to distrust. I witnessed abuse and was abused, rejected, and abandoned for many years by the family in which I grew up and the family that was created around me. It was not unusual for me to see my mother with bruises from the anger that enveloped the walls of abuse in my family.

My mother was powerless against her abusive husbands, but *I* was powerless against *her* abuse. A phrase that my mother branded into my brain was, "You are a terrible child. I can't take you anywhere." I never knew how I was a *terrible child*, but I felt very alone much of the time. I came to believe that was why no one wanted to be around me. I now know that it had nothing to do with me and everything to do with my mother's own orientation of life. My mother was the type of woman who would anger quickly, and her revenge was quite covert at times. She thrived by pitting people against each other so that she would look good and get what she wanted.

I learned at an early age that no one could be trusted, except for my grandmother, who always attempted to protect me as much as she could. She always drove me to school in the morning and was there to pick me up at the end of the day. Other kids made fun of me by saying, "We don't want to play with you. You have to live with your grandma." Then they'd laugh and make faces at me, but my grandma was always there to wipe my tears and cuddle me with her love.

Many of the neighborhood girls weren't allowed to play with me when I lived with my grandparents because of the chaos and fear that was generated by what was going on in my life with my family. So many drunk people going in and out of my grandparents' home and the police coming late in the evenings to either remove my father or stepfather from the premises did not make way for friendships with children who did not live in that type of environment.

I do know that it was my grandmother who held the magic of love in her heart and soothed the fear and sadness in my heart. She spent her days and nights attempting to coddle me from the cruelties of my environment by sweetly telling me, "I love you, sweetheart."

As a child, I spent much time alone. At times, my grandmother was able to convince my mother to leave me with her so I wouldn't have to go to my mother's house and be part of the craziness. Whenever I called my grandma and asked her to get me after I had been forced to go with my mother, she was always there. I sat up in trees, often trying to escape the words, the crazy loudness of the drunken parties, the extreme abuse that was still visible through the trees, and the cries and the screams of the abused.

When I was a little girl, my mother seemed to take great pleasure in combing my long blonde hair after she had washed it. My hair was very fine and soft, and it would be full of snarls and tangles. My mother would shout, "Stand still now; quit moving around!"

I hated it when she combed my hair. "Ouch, Mommy! Stop! You're pulling my hair," I would cry out, with tears running down my cheeks.

She always started at the crown of my head and jerked and pulled the snarls and tangles until I would cry. "Please, Mommy, stop. It hurts, it hurts!"

But she would be angry because I was squirming in pain. She yelled at me, "Shut up and stand still, or it's going to take longer and it will really hurt!" Oh, how I cried. Angrily, she would scream, "Stop crying, or I'll give you something to cry about. I'm going to comb this hair if it's the last thing I do!"

It hurt so bad, and my hair came out on the comb as my little head throbbed from her sadistic enjoyment of this ruthless treatment of me.

In first grade, when I was five, I took a pair of scissors and cut my own hair so my mother couldn't hurt me anymore. She always braided my hair and put it in pigtails. I dreaded it each time, as she would pull it so tight that the sides of my face were pulled back.

On this particular day, after one such attack on my hair again, I stood in front of the mirror as I was getting ready for school. I looked into the mirror, saw my reflection, and a thought came into my mind: *I'm going to stop her from hurting me anymore.* I found a pair of scissors in the bathroom drawer and proceeded to cut off one of the pigtails.

Just then, she stormed into the bathroom, grabbed the scissors from my hand, and screamed, "You're going to school just like that, and I hope everyone likes your new haircut!" She grabbed my arm above the elbow, squeezing so hard it hurt, and marched me to the car to drive me to school.

I was humiliated. I thought I would be taken to the beauty shop to get my hair cut, but instead, she made me go to school that way. I begged her, "Please don't make me go to school. Please don't make me go to school like this. Take me to get my hair cut."

She just laughed and said, "I hope you like your hair now. This is what you wanted!"

I tried to wear a scarf to conceal the hideousness of my appearance, but my teacher said, "Celeste, you need to take off your scarf. You cannot wear a scarf in school."

I pleaded with her to let me wear it, but she made me remove it. My classmates laughed at me and made fun of me all day. I was so embarrassed.

After school, my mother picked me up and said, "Get in. We're going to get all your hair cut off." She then drove me to the beauty salon where she went for her haircuts, and the beautician gave me a very short haircut. My mother never hurt me again by tearing that comb through my hair.

From time to time, my mother would move back to my grandparents' when the abuse she received became too extreme. It was only for a short while, and then she would return to the man she was married to again, into the arms of the abuser, another like the first one. When she stayed with us, she had the upstairs bedroom, and I always slept in my grandmother's bed with her. My grandfather had a separate bedroom; he and my grandmother exchanged no intimacy.

When my mother was there, I would go upstairs when she came home from work and watch her dress to go uptown to the bars. She was very pretty and always dressed very stylishly—usually a dress, high heels, and sometimes a hat. She never stayed home and rarely ate dinner with us. When we were alone, I would say, "Mom, will you stay home and spend some time with me tonight?"

She would just say, "No, I have plans tonight."

I felt so sad, knowing that she didn't want to be with me. I wanted her to love me. She was never loving toward me but also never hurt me when I was around my grandmother. Sometimes I would cry because I was so sad, and Grandma would rock me in the rocking chair and softly whisper, "I love you, honey." I knew she really did. She was the only one I could count on for love and safety.

My parents divorced when I was seven years old, and my mother started dating another man. One day she excitedly said, "I'm dating Elvis Presley." She was a huge fan of Elvis, and I was so excited to meet him. We had many of his records—45s and albums. I remember having a plastic guitar and pretending I was Elvis Presley; I sang to his music. Imagining that she was dating Elvis Presley was the most exciting thing ever! I remember that first Christmas when I met him. I wrapped a package of gum and put a sticker on it that read, "To Elvis."

Sadly, my fantasy ended the first time I saw him drunk, beating my mother, when I was seven years old. There were glass French doors opening to their bedroom, and he threw her through the glass. I stood there, terrified, as I watched her have a nervous breakdown on their bed that night. He ran out of the house. I was crying and kept saying to him, "Please don't leave. Help my mom. Please help my mom!" I begged him to come back. I didn't know what to do!

Finally, he returned, and the "honeymoon" period started again. At this time, they had not even married yet.

This incident was quite a minor one compared to some of the beatings I witnessed. My father was even more brutal than this man—and this man was horrible. I remember beatings from when I was just a toddler until the time of my parents' divorce, when I had been in grade school for two years. I remember very few other things about my life until I was ten years old. From that point, I remember everything, especially the continuous beatings she received.

I was always so frightened. After living such a terrifying life—with my biological father beating my mother and always fearing for her life as well as mine—here we were again. I could never understand any of this craziness and anger.

Whenever my mother was angry, her eyes would glare at me, and her lips would tighten, with all the muscles in her face ready to explode, as if there were volcanic eruptions happening under the surface. Her voice was extremely condescending, with the roar of a lion that would send fear, like lightning bolts, racing down my arms and legs in a fight-flight-or-freeze response. I would attempt to run from her, but she would scream at me and grab my hair and jerk on it. That was always the first thing she would go for when she was angry—my hair. When she was in a fit of rage, if I was able to get out of arm's reach, she would throw her shoes at me. She just took a shoe off her foot and nailed me with it when she was angry that life was not going her way. Vengeance was her mode of action, and her narcissism always operated with a payback response. I walked on eggshells around her and my stepfather. I could never say anything to him because I was told it could cause him to drink. His moods would change like flipping a light switch on and off, and so would hers.

It is because of the fear of loss that children do not come forward with this tragic behavior imposed upon them, and it is the fear of loss that continues to keep them connected to the abuser, especially the narcissistic abuser. A child's point of reference is diminished due to lack of sociability and knowledge of the world and its behaviors.

I was the child in school who sat and stared out the window. It was extremely difficult for me to concentrate. The teachers would call on me to answer a question, and I had no idea what they were even asking. I would just mumble, "I'm sorry. I don't know the answer."

Away from school, my life was traumatic, and there was no escape. I started seeing school counselors in junior high school, due to my inattentiveness, but it was the brutality happening in my mother's home that crippled my ability to focus. I never trusted the counselors enough to tell them the real story of why I couldn't concentrate in school. I really don't know how I made it through school; I will address this as I journey on.

Sometimes on weekends, I had to go to my stepgrandparents' home in the country. It was quite primitive, with an outdoor pump attached to a windmill, from which we filled containers for drinking water. There was no indoor plumbing, which meant restroom facilities were out past the garage, next to a dense row of trees, in the form of an old wooden outhouse. Toilet paper hung on a rusty spike that was pounded into the bare, rotted siding of the weathered wall.

On these weekends, large amounts of alcohol were always consumed by all who were there, including my grandfather, my stepgrandparents, my mother, my stepfather and his sister and her husband, and sometimes my aunt and uncle. They played poker all day and night. Everyone was so loud and argued about the cards that were played. My grandfather took the longest time to shuffle the cards and deal them out. During his drunken dialogue, those playing with him often got irritated because the shuffle or even the deal took so long. He often stopped, and his words slurred as he said, "Just a sad second, son." Then he went on with whatever verbiage tumbled out of his drunken mouth.

Some laughed at him, but others were annoyed, especially my stepfather.

After consuming an enormous amount of whiskey, my stepfather became very violent. He'd accuse someone at the table of doing some sort of act that he didn't like. It really didn't matter which person it was. His personality changed like Jekyll and Hyde. He'd start an argument by pushing or slapping the target of his anger, and this would escalate into a fist fight. The moment I saw this behavior starting, I left the house. Sometimes they broke windows and even furniture.

I never stayed in the house when I recognized the energy ramping up to these fights. I could feel myself panicking with fear and shouted inside my head, *I'm scared! Have to leave. Climb a tree. Need to be safe.* I was too young to do anything about the anger in a setting like that, so I went into hiding. I always heard them because the kitchen door was open, letting out all the smoke from their cigarettes. I always saw them, but they never knew where I was—nor did they care.

I would sit up in the trees most of the time and look down into the kitchen window and door. I could see everything that happened. I heard the shouting and screams from my stepgrandparents' home. My stepfather always started the fight and struck first. Before my mother met him, he had been in the army and had fought in the Korean War. He was very aggressive, especially when drinking, and he drank every day. I will describe one such evening and the insanity of what happened.

On this particular evening, they sat around the kitchen table at my stepgrandparents' home, playing cards. I watched as each person got drunker as time went by. My stepfather's sister turned to him and said, "Are you drinking all the whiskey?"

He looked at her with daggers in his eyes. "What the fuck are you talking about?" His anger had begun to rage, and he slapped her alongside her face, knocking her off her chair and onto the floor.

Her husband jumped up and told my stepfather, "Hey, what the hell do you think you are doing, hitting my wife?" He walked over to help her up.

My stepfather then pushed him and punched him in the face. I was in the kitchen doorway at the time and ran out the back door. I then stood peering in through the side kitchen window. I was so scared that I didn't know what to do. I was crying and shaking and felt completely helpless. I didn't know where to go—there were no nearby neighbors.

My mother's father stood up, and my stepfather pushed him to the floor. My mother tried to help her father get up, and my stepfather slapped her and pushed her against the table. My stepfather's sister was now up and screaming at him, and so was her husband. My stepfather punched her husband and knocked him through the kitchen window. Everyone was screaming and crying. My stepfather ran out the door to the car.

My mother ran after him, calling his name and yelling, "Wait! I'm coming with you. Wait, wait! I'm coming with you!" She then screamed, "Celeste, Celeste, get over here right now. We're leaving!"

He started driving; she got the car door open, and I came running. He barely stopped for me to get in. I could not even imagine what would happen from there.

I experienced a terrifying ride home on dark, narrow gravel roads. My stepfather's erratic driving had us swerving on the gravel, and at one time, I looked at the speedometer and it read ninety miles an hour. All I could do was sink onto the floor in the back seat of the car and cry to myself. I was so afraid to say a word and terrified that he would crash the car.

The vehicle plowed through ruts on the road, and my mother screamed, "Slow down, slow down!" When this happened, the car abruptly stopped.

He looked at her and yelled, "Do you want to drive?" She fearfully said no. He slapped her and said, "Then keep your damn mouth shut!"

Off we raced again.

When we arrived home, he got out of the car and slammed the door shut. My mother ran after him. No one ever thought about me in all of this. I kept very quiet and walked into the house and into my bedroom. I could hear them yelling at each other. I came out and saw him push her through the doorway and onto the floor. He jumped on top of her and started slapping her across the face.

I screamed and cried and said, "Get off my mom! Leave her alone, leave her alone!" I ran to the telephone to call the sheriff, but he jumped up and pulled the phone off the wall. I ran from the house, down the tar road—we lived in the country at this time—and pounded on the neighbor's door.

When they answered, I was crying and told them, "Ken is beating my mom. I have to call the sheriff."

The neighbor said, "I will call the sheriff for you."

His wife and children tried to calm me down, but I was traumatized. I waited until I saw the sheriff pull into our driveway before leaving for home. I had no idea what I would find when I walked through the door. I hid in the bathroom so my stepfather would not see me. He was escorted out of the house by the sheriff; then I came out of the bathroom. My mother was standing in the kitchen, blood on her face, her blouse ripped, and she was crying. She just said, "Go to your room and go to bed."

A few days later, he was back at home and the honeymoon period began yet again. My mother swooned over him, black eye and all.

Periodically, he would go to treatment for alcohol dependence but always relapsed shortly after returning home. Sometimes, he would brag, "We get liquor sneaked in on the treatment grounds; visitors smuggle it in for us!" He would laugh, and my mom would say, "You better not get caught."

My stepfather was a very angry man, and I wondered why this was. One evening, his parents were laughing, during a card party at their country home, about giving my stepfather liquor when he was ten years old and laughing at his drunken behavior. He had been an alcoholic since he was a young child, and his parents thought it was funny at that time.

These are just a few of my very vivid memories. If I were to relive each incident that I witnessed—the beatings my mother received and the horror that I experienced—I wonder if my fragile psyche would survive. Once was enough for even one of the events that I witnessed and the many times when I didn't know if I would live or die. Never did anyone ask how I was doing. I never talked about what happened in my home, except to my grandmother. I was too afraid.

Even though we had ample money to live very comfortably and have the niceties of life, it was wasted by the violence that surrounded my childhood. I likened myself to what author David Pelzer coined the "Lost Child" in his eye-opening account of his childhood. Although I was not neglected and abused to the sadistic lengths he had been, I was one of the lost children.

From my earliest recollection, I had the role of caretaker when I was with my mother, as she did not know how to take care of herself. I cleaned for her and did whatever she thought needed attention at the time. My payment was in lavish gifts that other kids longed for but that would be taken from me at any time without warning. I was the only child I knew who, at age ten, had my own television in my bedroom, a clock radio (which were new on the market then), and stylish clothing, with shoes and a purse to match my outfits.

When I was ten, I also was given a Welsh pony named Champ. He was taller than a pony but not as large as a horse. Champ was a pinto; the dominant color of his coat was brown with patches of white and black. He had some very undesirable habits, one being that he would walk around the corner of the house and buck me off. I would run in the house, crying, and my stepdad would take me outdoors and sit me right back on Champ, only to be bucked off again. That pony was just not a pony to be ridden, and when my parents finally realized this, Champ was trained to pull a two-wheeled cart, and I never rode him again.

The next summer, I was sent to stay with my great-aunt, who lived about three hundred miles south of my home; this happened for a few summers in a row. I stayed with her for a few weeks because that is what my mother would do—send me somewhere so she wouldn't have to take care of me. Then she and my stepdad could drink without me being in the way.

When I arrived home after a visit with my great-aunt one summer, there was a new horse for me in the pasture, a white Arabian mare. I named her Dolly Jean, and she became my best friend. I had her in one horse show and loved it; I loved her.

My mother's volatile temper occurred without warning. Seldom did she talk to me; if she did, it usually ended with rash, condescending remarks. Once, when I was eleven, I was going out to ride my horse, and as I walked through the kitchen, my mother hollered at me, "Where do you think you're going, Lady Jane?"

I already knew her anger was escalating because she called me *Lady Jane* when things were not going her way. "I'm going out to ride my horse," I replied.

She rose from her chair and yelled, "Oh no, you're not! You have ironing to do. You're not going anywhere!"

"Can I do it later?" I asked.

"Get back in here right now, and take care of that ironing!"

"I just want to ride my horse for a little bit."

She lunged toward me but missed me, so she grabbed her shoe from foot and hit me with it. I ran, but she ran after me, grabbed my long hair, and jerked me to the floor.

I was crying and screamed, "Stop! You are hurting me!"

She said, "Get back in there and do your ironing, or you're not going anywhere."

I got up and walked into the dining room, still crying, and began ironing.

My mother ordered me to do things for her constantly. She gave me five dollars a week for an allowance if I cleaned the whole house for her. If I didn't do everything she wanted done, there was no allowance. She never asked, and she never said thank you.

After a night of living in fear, as my stepfather came home drunk and beat on my mother, I would experience trauma overload—mentally, emotionally, and physically. I was unable to focus in a functional manner in school. At times, my mother and stepfather would leave for work in the mornings, and I would stay home from school. When they came home for their half-hour lunch, I would hide out in the barn until they left for work again. I wrote my own notes for the principal's office to excuse my absence when I returned to school; it wasn't questioned because my mother and I had the same handwriting.

My stepfather used embarrassingly sexual language around my girlfriends. He would make comments about them having sexy bodies or beautiful hair. The neighbor girl and I were close friends, and one sunny afternoon, as we sat in the backyard, he came out with a drink in his hand. He always drank whiskey, and it didn't take long before his intoxication was obvious. He smiled inappropriately at my girlfriend and said, "I bet you would be nice to lie down with."

My friend looked at me and said, "I have to go, Celeste."

The anger I felt toward him was unforgiving. I stayed away from him as much as possible after that. My friends stopped coming over because they felt threatened by him, and so did I.

One summer morning, as my mother sat in a lawn chair in the yard, and I was playing with my dog, Duke, my stepfather walked over to us. He had been drinking quite a bit already that day. He looked at me, laughed, and said, "Your ass is as wide as ten ax handles!"

I was astonished by this. After he said that, I wore clothing for decades that covered my backside. I was twelve years old at the time, tall, and thin. I never saw myself as that young thin girl again; his words made me into a freak that day that no one would ever want.

As mentioned, I had a pony and a horse from the time I was ten to twelve years old. My Welsh pony didn't like my stepfather. My pony was standing in his stall, and my stepfather tried to put a saddle on him. My pony turned his head and tried to bite him. Instantly, my stepfather turned around and punched my pony in the mouth, causing him to bleed. I was crying and yelled, "Stop! Don't hurt him! Stop, stop!"

My stepfather said, "Shut the fuck up, and get out of here!"

I ran from the barn and hid in the pasture. I didn't know what to do. He was not nice to either my pony or my horse.

My white Arabian, Dolly Jean, had given birth to many colts, I was told, before she found her home with me. She gave birth to two beautiful foals when I had her. Our pasture had two gates, one smaller gate and another that was wide enough to bring a hayrack through it. Dolly did not like the big gate, for some reason; she was afraid of it, so I never took her through it.

My mother and stepfather were working in the yard in the afternoon in late summer, and I had Dolly saddled up; I had been riding. My stepfather walked toward me, took the reins from my hand, and told me to get down. He got on Dolly and started walking her toward the large gate. Suddenly, Dolly stopped and would not go through it.

I told him she did not like that gate, but he yelled, "Shut up!" He tried to get her to go through it again, and this time, she reared up on her hind legs.

I shouted, "Stop! She doesn't want to go through there. Please stop!"

He was swearing at her and me and tried to take her through the gate again. This time, she reared up straight in the air and fell over backward on him.

I started screaming, but he said, "Shut up, goddamn it, shut up." He got off the ground and started whipping my horse. I ran, crying, into the shed where we kept the tack. I didn't know what to do. I jumped on a saddle that was on a saddle stand, and the saddle and I both fell to the floor. A spike nail ran up my back, and it was painful. The wound was bleeding, but I couldn't tell anyone. I went into the house and tried to clean my back and put a bandage on it. I never told anyone about what happened. I didn't talk to my mother or my stepfather for a long time after that incident.

Living in that environment was like living in the Twilight Zone. I was uncertain of my every move, every day. *What will today bring?* I wondered; it was always unknown.

My mother and stepfather decided that we would take a vacation to the Black Hills in South Dakota, and they gave me permission to take a friend on the trip. I asked a younger girlfriend who lived next door. She was quite excited. I knew that if something happened, I would have someone to be with.

Driving down a tar road somewhere in South Dakota my stepfather, who had been drinking on the trip, started an argument with my mother. The truck camper he was driving came to a screeching halt. My friend and I were in the camper portion of the truck, and we were getting scared. My stepfather got out of the truck, went to the passenger side, and pulled my mother out onto the road.

My friend and I jumped out and stood there, shaking. He looked at us angrily and yelled, "Get the hell out of the way!" We scrambled to my mother's side and stood there, watching him. He went to the back of the camper, climbed in, and threw our luggage out onto the tar road, yelling, "Here's your shit. Enjoy your vacation!"

We were all crying and didn't know what to do. He climbed back into the truck and drove off. There we stood, next to our suitcases, with no idea where we were or what to do. My mother finally said, "Just get your suitcases and start walking." So we did.

As we walked, we saw the truck coming back down the road. He stopped and said, "Get your asses in here."

My mom said, "Just put your belongings in the camper, girls." We did, and off we drove. When we stopped at a campground for the night, he just went to bed.

My girlfriend never came to my house again. She was eleven, and I was twelve years old.

I lived a roller-coaster existence. I never knew from one minute to the next what was going to happen. It was summer again. I was out by the barn with my horse, Dolly, and my dog, Duke, when a truck with a horse trailer attached pulled into the yard. My parents came out and greeted the driver.

The driver said, "Well, here he is. Let me get him unloaded." I watched as he backed a beautiful buckskin gelding out of the trailer. I walked over to the trailer, and my stepdad handed me the lead with a proud look on his face. "Here's your new horse," he said, "His name is Buck."

I couldn't believe it! I was so happy. I loved horses more than anything; he was a quarter horse. "Thank you, thank you, thank you," I said. "I love him!"

The man who delivered Buck shook hands with my stepdad, got in the truck, and drove off. I kept petting my new horse, and the honeymoon period began again with these two emotionally and mentally ill people, who thought this was what parenting was all about.

One day after arriving home from school—I was thirteen years old at the time—I hurried to change from my school clothes to go out to the barn to see Buck.

"Don't bother going to the barn," my mother sneered. I turned to look at her, feeling stunned. Looking me straight in the eye, she said, "I sold your horse today."

I was completely devastated; my world came crashing down around me. "How could you do that?"

"You're never here anyway."

I looked at her and screamed, "You are not my mother, and you never have been!"

After that, any perceived connection I had with her crumbled. *She has never taken care of me*, I realized at that moment. *She has never protected me, only put my life in danger over and over again, and I have never been able to trust her!*

After that, I went back to my grandmother's.

I have no idea how I made it through school; most of it was a blur. I had a gifted mind; learning and creativity came easily to me, and even though I felt so lost, I had drive, a resilience that was inherent.

I played clarinet, accordion, and guitar and enjoyed playing around with the piano. In fourth grade, my teacher talked to my mother about accelerating me to sixth grade and skipping fifth grade, but she would not agree. I was already young in my classes because I had started school earlier than most of the other kids. I graduated at age seventeen, younger than most others.

My mother and stepfather sold the home in the country after selling my horse and moved into town when I was thirteen years old. Their marriage continued to be an abusive circus of beatings and honeymoon periods. I was in ninth grade at the time, and living with her was a continuous on-and-off cycle. I walked home from school one fall day, and, much to my astonishment, my mother had moved. I looked in the windows and saw that the house was empty. I didn't know what to think or do.

I walked to a friend's house and told her, "When I got home from school, I didn't live there anymore. All the furniture was gone, and I don't know what happened."

She tried to comfort me, and when I felt calmer, I called my grandmother. "Grandma, I don't know what happened, but I don't live where I did when I went to school this morning."

Grandma said, "Where are you? I will come to get you. Your mother is here."

Soon after the call, I was on my way to my grandmother's again.

Shortly thereafter, my mother and stepfather, in one of the honeymoon periods again, bought a triplex. My great-aunt, with whom my mother had lived from ages twelve to seventeen, moved upstairs. I had a two-room apartment off the side of the house, and my mother and stepfather lived in the large apartment on the main floor. Their apartment had only one bedroom; thus, the reason why I had the small apartment. I loved the privacy and being away from their drinking and fighting.

My last recollection of living with my stepfather and mother was a devastating sight. I heard yelling and crying as I entered the house. I was fifteen years old and was at the end of my days of living with my mother yet again. I ran into her bedroom and saw her lying on her back on the bed, with my stepfather sitting on top of her, with his knees pinning her arms down. She was yelling and trying to wriggle loose from his hold, but she could not.

He held a pair of leather gloves and was continuously slapping her across the face with them as he said, "You bitch, I should kill you!"

I yelled at him, "Leave my mom alone! Get off her right now!"

He looked at me and jumped off the bed. He came angrily toward me, screaming, "Shut the fuck up!"

In a flash, a superhuman strength came over me, and I grabbed his arm and flung him from the bedroom into the dining room, which was adjacent to their bedroom. He hit his head on the stereo—it was on a stand in the dining room. It fell on him and knocked him out. I ran to the cupboard and grabbed a butcher knife, and when he came to, I was standing next to him with the knife. I screamed, "Get the hell out of here and never come back!"

My mother was standing there, crying. "Be careful, Celeste!"

My stepfather crawled to his knees and then stood up.

I screamed, "Get out, or I will kill you!"

He stumbled to the door, went out to his car, and drove off. He never came back again, except with the sheriff to get his clothing. I slept with that butcher knife under my pillow every night for a long time.

Another of the Many Childhood Moves

> A child of the wind, blowing, swirling,
> a path never planned,
> Whirling, twirling wherever will she land

In the spring of 1965, when I was in tenth grade, my mother came home one day and said, "I saw a psychiatrist today, and he told me that if I got rid of my husband and my daughter, I would be fine." She told me that she was sending me to live with my father and stepmother, who lived in a large southwestern city.

I was shocked and crushed. I begged her, "Please do not send me to my dad's. I don't even know him!" I cried and pleaded with her but she told me, "Get your things packed; you're going!"

The next day, she told me that my father's parents were driving me down there.

My paternal grandparents were quite old, and my grandfather was very hard of hearing. Whenever he did not want to hear my grandmother, he would turn off his hearing aid and couldn't hear a thing. The drive was very scary. On the Kansas City Turnpike, we drove twenty-six miles out of our way because he had his hearing aid turned off and didn't hear my grandmother tell him where his turn was; he just drove past it. The next exit was thirteen miles farther, and when he came to it, he had to turn around and drive back to the exit he'd missed. Another time, he attempted to press on the brakes, but his other foot was under the brake pedal. He had to veer off onto the shoulder of the road so that we didn't hit the stopped cars in front of us until he could get his foot free.

I was a nervous wreck. We stopped that night at a motel. I said to my grandmother, "I am so scared of Grandpa's driving that I feel sick."

She said, "It's not that bad; he just doesn't hear sometimes."

"I refuse to get back in the car with you. I would like some of my money to buy a bus ticket for the rest of the trip." She tried to talk me out of it, but I cried and begged her to help me. Finally, I called my mother, and she agreed that my grandmother should give me the money for a bus ticket.

I took the rest of my journey with Greyhound.

Much to my surprise, a day after I arrived, my grandparents pulled up in front of the house.

It wasn't long after my arrival that I found out my dad was still drinking. Living with my dad, though, allowed me to experience a new independence. I could smoke cigarettes in front of him, and even though I didn't have a driver's license, he still gave me the keys to the car, and I could drive.

My father was a butcher for a large food chain. He worked during the day and was home only occasionally at night. My stepmother worked evenings—I don't remember what her job was—and didn't arrive home until after midnight during the week.

One night, my father came home drunk. I was in bed when he stumbled into my bedroom, turned on the light, and sat down on my bed. He started to talk to me like I was five years old. I was scared.

He had his face close to mine and slurred his words. "Are you doing your chores? You better be doing your part around here. I let you come here and live, and you better appreciate what I am doing for you."

My stepbrother was trying to get him out of my bedroom because he knew I was terrified; he also knew what my father was capable of doing when he was drunk. Finally, my dad left my room, and my other stepbrother and stepsister came in and sat with me as I lay there crying; they too were frightened.

My oldest brother said in a very low voice, "He gets abusive when drunk."

After that, I was fearful of my dad and did not trust him. I made a point of staying out of his way.

My father remained an abusive alcoholic, and one evening, he came home drunk when my stepmother was working. Only my three stepsiblings and I were at home. One stepbrother was a year older than me; and the other two were younger. My stepsister was the youngest. We had the door locked and knew he was drunk.

He was yelling and swearing, pounding on the door, and threatening us. "Let me in, or I will break down this goddamn door!"

We were so scared. I was shaking as we ran out the front door. Just then, we heard him breaking in the back door. My stepsiblings and I huddled together under a large evergreen tree until my stepmother came home from work, which was after midnight.

When she saw us, she said, "What happened? What's going on?"

I said, "Dad came home drunk and broke down the back door. He was very angry!"

She went to a neighbor's and called her parents. She told them what was going on, and they came right away and took us back to their house to stay that night.

The next morning, she made airline reservations for me to fly back to the Midwest and return to my mother's home. She also called the high school to say I would no longer be attending. Then she and her father drove me to the airport.

My stepmother said, "I will ship your clothes and guitar after I can get back into the house."

She had run in fear of her life that night with us children. I didn't grasp what was happening; everything moved so quickly. My grandfather, with whom I had lived, would not accept a collect call from me, and I could not find my mother. So there I was, on an airplane, flying back home, and no one knew I was coming.

It was eighty-six degrees the day my flight left in March, so my attire was a sundress and sandals; no jacket or sweater. The airline had a layover for an hour, and I was finally able to reach my grandmother.

She said, "I told your grandfather that I was accepting your call." She was shocked when I told her what had happened and where I was. "I will try to find your mother and tell her where you are."

She didn't make plans, however, for my arrival back home. When the plane finally landed in my home state, snow covered the ground, and it was very cold—the temperature was in the teens. Again, I wore nothing but a sundress and sandals.

I called my grandmother. She had not found my mother and said, "I don't know what to do." My grandparents were quite old at the time and were unable to rescue me. All night long, I sat in the airport, trying to contact my mother. Finally, about 3:00 a.m., she answered the phone. I quickly told her what had happened. She and her then-boyfriend arrived at the airport a little after 5:00 a.m. I was fifteen years old, scared, and alone.

My mother walked up to me wearing my pretty red winter coat and handed me an old jacket she had grabbed before she left to pick me up. That had been my first experience with living in the Southwest and another notch in my trauma belt.

During the time I was living with my biological father, my mother had separated from my stepfather. When I returned home again, she was living in a very small one-bedroom house behind my great-aunt's home. The living room became my bedroom; I slept on the couch. I'd grown accustomed to the freedom of living at my father's, but when I lit up a cigarette one day in front of my mother, she said, "Put that cigarette out!"

I adamantly stated, "I could smoke at my dad's, and I will smoke around you too."

She didn't reply, and nothing more was said about my smoking. I had no respect for her and what she said. I felt that she had betrayed me throughout my entire life and had no love or care for me at all. I was just something she had to put up with from time to time.

My great-aunt, who owned the house my mother was renting, was also an alcoholic and lived with her boyfriend. They fought and drank; that was it. My great-aunt was very good to me, though, and supported me in any way she could.

One morning, when I woke up at my grandmother's house, I overheard her and my great-aunt talking. They mentioned my aunt's previous boyfriend and how jealous he had always been. She had lived in a large brick apartment building downtown on the third floor when they had been together. I remembered it well—small, with one bedroom, a living room that overlooked the busy street, and a kitchen and bathroom. Small businesses rented the main floor so there was always lots of activity in the area. Next door to her building was a small, intimate café that was quite famous for their sandwiches—my favorite place to eat when I was young.

They talked quietly in my grandmother's living room about the day a parade was held in town, and the parade route went right past her apartment building. My aunt said, "I was standing at the window, watching the parade, and all of a sudden, there was a gunshot. The bullet hit right next to me on the outside of the window."

As she and my grandmother spoke, there was sadness in her voice that I still remember. It was her ex-boyfriend who had shot the gun and tried to kill her. Miraculously, he had been unsuccessful, and she did not press charges. He did go to jail, though; I remembered that but nothing more.

I was always reminded of the horrors of alcoholism all around me. At night, when the lights were out and I would try to sleep, the nightmares began. They were always the same; I was filled with fear and couldn't get away.

Many other men were involved in my mother's life when she wasn't married, and a role model for a healthy relationship or marriage did not exist. Sometimes, she would have some new man pick her up at Grandma's, and she would introduce him to everyone, and then off she'd go.

These men usually had something memorable about them. One was married, and they would go away and have weekend affairs. It wasn't until I met his wife at church while with my mother that I felt the shame of her behavior. Another had horses, and one was a city official, but I remember one particular story the most. My mother was seeing a man who had a parrot. She laughed as she told me, "That damn parrot just wouldn't stop talking, and Rob told it to shut up. The bird got really noisy, running around its cage, and Rob reached in and grabbed the bird and ripped the head off it. It was quiet then!"

I was in shock. I have not forgotten this man. Whenever he showed up, I went into another room. I was afraid of him. I saw him as a scary man; if he would be that awful to his parrot, what would he do to another person? The gripping thought was that my mother saw that as somewhat amusing.

Abandonment and rejection ran rampant in my family. Many divorces and many stepmothers, stepfathers, stepsiblings, and extended family members. My mother seemed to enjoy it when she could hurt others. It was impossible to explain my relationship to someone when referring to family members.

I was happy that my brother lived a block away from my grandparents while I was growing up. I would go to his house quite often. He had two younger half brothers, and

I would play with them. His stepmother and father were usually pretty nice to me. My brother and I were eight years apart in age, so we had little in common, but I loved music and would go up to his bedroom and listen to his stereo. There was a train set in another room, and I loved playing with that. My brother was gone most of the time, either to school, working, or at a friend's house. But he was still my brother, and sometimes, he'd come down to Grandma's, and we'd see each other then as well. He was always good to me.

In 1965, when I was fifteen years old, I dated a young man who was eighteen years old and lived in a neighboring town. He played drums and was in a band that periodically played on weekends in the surrounding area. After we'd been dating for about eight months, he enlisted in the armed forces. The Vietnam War was mounting in the mid-1960s, and there were rumors of the draft being activated. He knew if he enlisted, he could choose the branch of the armed forces in which he would serve.

We'd met at a popular teenage dance club in my hometown and were smitten by each other at first glance. The hippie movement was slowly finding its way to the Midwest, and he was the first young man in the area with long hair, a mustache, and a beard. His clothing resembled more of a beatnik style—tight corduroy pants and turtleneck shirts. He was what I deemed as pretty cool. All the other girls swooned around him, but he only had eyes for me.

We always had so much fun together. He was not only my boyfriend but my friend. One evening, he took me to a concert at a well-known ballroom in our area, where the nationally known group the Byrds were playing. It was so exciting, and afterward, my boyfriend and I met David Crosby and Roger McGuinn. We had the opportunity to talk a bit, but I don't remember the conversation—I was starstruck! It was thrilling for me!

We always had some kind of adventure, and we loved to dance and laugh and did both quite often. He also knew about the nature of my living conditions, my mother and stepfather, and the beatings that occurred. I felt safe with him and knew he loved me.

He was such a great support in my life, and I came to depend on him for so much. It was very important to him that I go to school and earn good grades. He told me, "Celeste, always pick your friends wisely. Be with the good guys." He would drive me to school when he stayed overnight at my house and would then drive back to his hometown. It was heartbreaking for me when he left for the service. I knew he would be back after boot camp, but that seemed like an eternity at the time.

One night, after we'd been dating for a while, we were "parking" out in the country, and he said, so very sweetly and softly, "If you love me, you will go all the way with me."

I was afraid that if I didn't, I would lose him. I was scared and didn't want to have sex with him but ended up doing so.

About a month later, he left for boot camp. Six weeks later, he came home from training, and we had sex again—and this time, I got pregnant. This is how it was for young girls, especially those who grew up as I did: you'd meet that special boy, and you'd believe this was someone who loved you, and you'd hope what he said was true.

I've worked with many adolescent girls in my career as a psychotherapist and many tell a similar story, not necessarily about the boy enlisting in the armed services but the story of loneliness, abuse at home, and a craving to be loved.

When I was pregnant, my mother told me that I had to give up my baby for adoption. She made arrangements for me to move into an unwed mothers' home in a large city, many miles from her. The stigma of pregnancy out of wedlock was disgraceful. The home was an old dark-brown brick building that loomed three or four stories high. It was quite intimidating to behold, and as I walked through the front door, I felt as if this was just another attempt to be rid of me. The environment was cold. The aged stark walls were compatible with the high, impersonal ceiling that towered above. I had just turned sixteen and was barely showing my pregnancy at the time.

When I was first admitted, I was provided a bed in a large dormitory with approximately twelve beds. Each side of the room had six beds with only a small wooden nightstand separating them. Each girl was allowed a small storage locker for personal belongings. Sadly, there was no privacy at all.

The girls in residence were multicultural. I'd come from a strictly white community, but I fit in surprisingly well with everyone. I kept to myself most of the time, though, because I was so unhappy and felt abandoned.

Sleeping in the dorm with no privacy made it easier for someone to steal your items at night, and it would be undetected. There were three rooms at the end of the dormitory. As time passed, a girl who resided in one of these more private rooms left the home, and I was invited by another who shared that room to move in. We had become friends prior to this, so I happily accepted. There were three of us in that room, and I felt safer with them.

There was a definite hierarchy in the group home. Some girls were quite dominant, the alpha females, and others, who were more passive, viewed them as leaders. They followed the strongest personality, who was always at the top of the totem pole. The environment was sad and impersonal. Trust was earned, not given.

I felt honored to be invited to move into the more private room with only two others. They were kind to me, and we developed a close friendship. We didn't associate with the others much; we stayed to ourselves. I attended school at the home so I wouldn't fall behind. I was to graduate from high school the next year, so it was important to me to attend classes.

Each of my new roommates was from a different culture, and we learned about each other as we spent many nights in our room, talking. Even so, I remained lonely and scared. I wasn't scared of my environment, but I felt rejected and abandoned again by my family and my boyfriend. Finally, my grandparents convinced my mother to allow me to leave the home and to live with them again. It was very shameful to be pregnant during that time, 1965–66, and my stepfather would not have me around.

I was now living with my grandparents and taking eleventh-grade classes at the high school in town. School started at 8:30 a.m., but my first class was at 7:00 a.m., and the next wasn't until 4:00 p.m. This was meant to provide me with an education while pregnant without my being around any of the other students—again, it was a shameful stigma to be pregnant and unmarried.

About two months after moving back in with my grandparents, I went into labor. I was taken to the hospital and placed in a room at the far end of the hall, away from the other patients, because of my age and my giving birth to an "illegitimate" child. My boyfriend did not know about any of this; I had not heard from him for several months. There was a shaming stigma inherent in society's values regarding pregnancy out of wedlock, which was shunned immensely, even in the hospital.

On the day when I was discharged from the hospital, I still hadn't been allowed to see my son. The nurses told me it would be too hard to give him up for adoption if I saw him, and I might want to back out of the adoption. My mother told me that if I did not give him up for adoption, I would have no life, that no one would ever want me. I succumbed to her continuous bullying.

I could not understand any of what was happening to me or my son—my home life, the stigma, the warnings from my mother, the incredible aloneness; it all played a devastating role in my life. The nurse came in with the discharge papers and told me that I could leave.

I said, "I'm not leaving the hospital until I can see my son."

My mother said sternly, "No, you're not going to see him. You'll just want to take him home and won't give him up for adoption."

I cried, "I'm not leaving this hospital without seeing my son!"

She finally agreed.

After what seemed like hours of waiting, I was taken to a small room, where a nurse was sitting in a chair, holding my baby son. I looked at him and asked to hold him.

The nurse refused. "I cannot let you hold him because you are giving him up for adoption."

As I gazed at him with tears in my eyes, I said through my tears, "I will always love you, and I will never forget you, Sean." I was then escorted out of the room and out of the hospital, with only the experience to haunt my life from that point on for a very long time.

Later in the summer, after the birth and adoption of my son, I went to live with my brother in a suburb of a large city in the upper Midwest. He was a teacher, and it was the best year of my life when I was living with him; it was my senior year of high school. His father did not want me living with my brother, and there were many arguments between them—some in front of me—but my brother stood his ground and kept me with him.

3

Early Adulthood

If you open the door and invite me in,
I will honor your vulnerability

After graduation from high school, I moved into the city. My first job, at age seventeen, was working for Northwestern Bell Telephone Company. I rented a studio apartment downtown and loved exploring the city. My boyfriend at the time, James, lived about three blocks from me, and we saw each other frequently. Life was going well, and I liked my new job and the people I was meeting.

James had moved to the same city where I was living when my brother and I lived together. He was a few months younger than me and worked in a dental lab, a small business with only a few employees. I believe his employer wanted to give him an opportunity because he had quit school but showed great promise. I was so proud of him, at age sixteen, showing up for work each day and living on his own in a small one-room apartment in the heart of the city.

We had been dating for about a year when we decided to move in together. I was so excited and asked, "In what area do you think we should look for an apartment?"

After searching newspaper ads, he said, "Let's look over by the park!"

I agreed. I loved the park. We rented a one-bedroom apartment in an old brownstone building across the street from the neighborhood park.

We went to the park often. The large oak trees formed umbrellas that shaded grassy areas—welcome rest for park dwellers looking for solitude. A few picnic tables were scattered about in no particular order. A small pond in the center of the park was home to a few ducks and geese that took over ownership of it during the warm-weather months. Tall green grasses surrounded most of the pond, and it was ecologically friendly for flying insects of numerous varieties. We lived only a few blocks from where we previously had lived, so walking to work, as we had done, was still an option.

In 1968, I sheepishly said to him one afternoon, "I have something to tell you."

He looked at me rather puzzled because I usually was quite direct in what I had to say but not this time. I sat down on the couch next to him and started to tear up. He was surprised and said, "What is it, Celeste? What is the matter?"

I then spoke through my tears. "I'm pregnant."

He looked at me curiously. Then he said, "How do you know?"

I explained, and we decided I needed to see a doctor. We promised we would go through this together, and we did.

A few months later, we moved to a nicer neighborhood in a residential area. A close girlfriend asked if she could live with us, and that helped tremendously with the rent because I could no longer work. Living together certainly had its ups and downs. My friend didn't like to wash dishes, and we would go several days, watching the dishes pile up, before anyone would wash them. We had many fights about the stinky, crusted dishes sitting in the sink and on the cupboard tops.

Finally, there was just too much bickering with our living arrangement, and the responsibilities of cohabitating weren't working. We all parted and each went our separate ways.

I was tired and irritable at times. Two of my long-time girlfriends from my hometown moved in with me for a couple of months before my baby was born and stayed with me for a month after I came home from the hospital. I then moved in with the girlfriend I had lived with when James had lived with us. It seemed like every few months, I was moving.

James and I still saw each other; we just didn't live together. On the day I went into labor, I called him at work and said, "I'm ready to have our baby. I'll meet you at the hospital." When I got there, however, I went right in for prepping and didn't see him until after our baby boy was born. He was there for us, just like he said he'd be.

I was in the hospital for seven days. That was at a time when insurance companies did not have the strict control they do now on how long a person could be hospitalized. I had my son with me every day and cared for him like all the other mothers around me did. I talked to him and named him right away. I told him, "I love you," all the time, knowing in my heart that I would not take him home with me.

My boyfriend and I were eighteen years old and had no idea how to take care of a baby, how to be parents, or how to support a baby. I was scared. I was afraid of failing. I didn't know what to do. We decided to wait before we made a decision. My heart was aching, so I placed our son in foster care for a month.

The day I left the hospital, I was alone. The nurse called a taxi for me, which took me home. When I got out of the taxi, I felt like I was in a world that I had never been in before. I walked into the apartment, and all of what I had been through hit me like a bag of boulders. I lay on my bed and cried. I was so depressed and heartbroken. At the end of the month, my two roommates moved out, and I was totally alone again for a short time.

James and I joined my mother and brother on a trip to Colorado for a week. I tried to have fun, but through it all, I kept thinking about my baby son. My brother didn't even know I had been pregnant because I had stayed away from him for a few months. (It was several years later before he learned about my pregnancy.)

After the vacation, my mother asked what I planned to do about my baby. When I told her I wasn't sure yet, she said to me, "I want to raise your baby as my own, and you can be the baby's 'sister.'"

My life flashed before my eyes, and I thought, *There is no way in hell that I will let you ruin another child."* Just the thought of it scared me so badly; I felt frozen in time. I knew I could not allow her to have control. I returned to my home in the city. I felt weak against her. She had ruined my life, and I knew if I kept my baby, she would do something to get him away from me. James and I knew what we had to do to save our child from having the type of life we both had grown up in. We decided to give up our baby for adoption. This broke my heart, but I didn't know what else to do or who to turn to.

The day I signed adoption papers, I gave up on me. My thoughts were, *I just gave birth to my second son. I am, once again in my life, placing another child for adoption.* I was seated across the table from a social worker who asked me many questions.

She compassionately asked, "How do you feel about giving up your baby for adoption?"

All I could say was, "I can't let another child be raised in the family I was raised in. My mother wants to raise him as her child, and she wants me to act as my son's sister. I'm afraid of what might happen to him if I take him home and she tries to take him away from me. She made me give up my first son for adoption, and I can't lose this child to her." I explained to the social worker about my mother's abuse toward me and her alcoholism. My head was spinning. I was old enough now to make my own decisions and was in an extremely sorrowful situation. I was so afraid of making the wrong decision.

She talked quickly. I had just spent seven days with my baby son Christian in the hospital, along with his visiting father, caring for him and loving him, knowing that would be all there was for us.

Christian was placed with Child Services and put in foster care until a home could be found for him. I did not fully understand the impact of this at the time. I only knew I was protecting him from the chemically dependent, abusive, narcissistic, highly dysfunctional family I had been born into.

The social worker looked at me with empathy in her eyes and said, "Celeste, please sign your name at the bottom of this document."

There it was, placed right in front of me, relinquishing all parental rights to my son. I was speechless. After I signed that document, I walked out of that office feeling as if I had just signed my life away.

The loneliness and despair I felt was overwhelming. My already fractured heart was crumbling within. There was no one at the door, waiting for me, as I stepped out of the cab that day. I knew then that I would be the one at the door some day for someone who was alone, whose heart was crying with no one to hear it.

Moving Forward

The road of many forks, another Lesson,
an uncertain sigh, another step

I decided to go to college, and it opened not only the doors to learning but also the door to destruction. I fell into a new world of alcohol and drugs; they became the mask to shield the pain I experienced. I was now nineteen years old and had no idea what my life even meant to me. I was drinking as often as I could, doing LSD, smoking marijuana, and popping Seconal. I was very much an activist and participated in protests and marches against the war in Vietnam and for civil rights. The hippie movement had spread across the country, and the environment was ripe for making change.

I was living, once again, with the girlfriend I had lived with prior to the birth of my second son. During this time, many people would just hang out in the park and play music. It was a magical era, and I found solace in just relaxing and listening to music.

One afternoon, I met a young man at the park. We enjoyed each other's company. He was fun to be around, and we started dating.

I was a frequent visitor to the neighborhood laundromat, and on one laundry day, I sat patiently in a chair, watching my clothes flop around in the dryer. Music played from a radio on a shelf above me, and I faded in and out of the words of the song I was listening to. I heard the door of the establishment open but did not bother to look up. Suddenly, a hand reached out to me—and there stood my beau. He had long ash-blond hair and blue eyes.

"Hi," I said, surprised to see him.

"Hello," he whispered. A smile spread across his face, and his eyes glistened as I took his hand. He swept me into his arms, and we danced around the washing machines that evening, laughing and being silly. The music, as if sensing our gaiety, swept us away.

This young man shared a beautiful relationship with me for a short time; it was at a time when I needed it most. I had ended the relationship I had with my second son's father and was rebuilding my life again. This positive man had the tools that helped me to do so.

The house where my girlfriend and I lived had become unsafe for us. One evening, as we sat listening to music, doing LSD, and drinking beer, my friend said, "Quick, Celeste, come here!" I ran over to the window where she was standing and saw a strange man walking around our house. My friend said, "He was looking in our window at us!"

We were both scared, and she called the police. Shortly thereafter, we moved.

After my first year of college, I quit school and moved in with three friends who lived in a small home next to a lake, outside of the city. We spent most of our time listening to music and using alcohol and drugs. Life continued to be meaningless to me. When I say I gave up on my life, I truly had given up. I was alone again and had quit caring about me.

In 1970, a couple of my housemates asked me one evening if I wanted to go to an outdoor rock concert in Wisconsin. I excitedly said, "Sure, that sounds awesome!" This concert occurred a year after Woodstock. We all jumped in my friend's van, bringing tents, lawn chairs, and food, and down the road we drove. The energy was so high that evening. We set up camp and stayed there for four days. The concert took place on a large farm, but all we could see was pastureland from where we were located. Thousands of people covered the hillside and grounds—eighty-five thousand, reportedly—and music echoed throughout the countryside.

The scene was incredible, with people dancing and singing to the music that thundered through the speakers from the stage. Paul Butterfield Blues Band, Buffy St. Marie, Ravi Shankar, and Steve Miller Band—just to name a few—set the mood for a drug party; you had to witness it to grasp the scope of what happened.

As I was stumbling back to my tent in the early morning hours of the second day, a man ran up and said, "The bikers are injuring people, and someone has been shot."

I was scared but extremely exhausted after being up all night. I stayed in the tent with my friends for a few hours and fell asleep. When I awoke, someone said, "The bikers have been run off." I was so relieved and walked back to where the stage was set up.

That evening, as I made my way up the hill, weaving between people and tents that were crammed together like puzzle pieces, I saw some familiar faces from my hometown. I stopped to say hello and to smoke a joint with them. I was introduced to a man who was very interesting to me. His name was William, and he wore a Captain America shirt and had a star painted on his face.

We talked about our lives, and I asked, "Are you attending college now?"

"I was," he said. "I just finished my first year at an all-male school, and I don't think I'm going back. I didn't like it."

"I just completed my first year in the city and also quit," I said.

We laughed and decided we would learn about life now instead of going to school. Although I didn't know it at the time, this man was to cross my path again in the near future and eventually become my husband.

The Quest for Self

Mirror, mirror on the wall,
only a fragment revealed.

For the first twenty years of my life—those that I remember; I have only a faint memory of childhood, except for the beatings I witnessed and running for my life—I had dreams of werewolves. I would awaken in the night, wet from sweating intensely because I was under the covers, hiding; in my dreams, a werewolf had been over my face, breathing down on me.

I went to the movies often when I was a child. At that time, horror flicks were quite popular, and the old movies with Lon Chaney as Wolfman and Bela Lugosi as Count Dracula were a big draw.

Even though I would see them often, I was scared to death as I watched them, sometimes covering my eyes with my fingers and plugging my ears with my thumbs. I started to experience nightmares, but the form the werewolf took was alarming to me.

Prior to my first marriage, my soon-to-be husband, William, two of our housemates, and I were tripping on LSD. We each sat in a different corner of the living room. As I looked around the room, I focused on William's face. His face turned into the face of a werewolf, then my father's face, then his face again. Back and forth it continued until I realized that the werewolf represented my father and my fear of him. After that experience, I talked to my husband about it and never had another dream like that again. I now know it was caused by trauma and my experiencing post-traumatic stress symptoms.

Not long after that night, we moved back to our hometown and started thinking about what we wanted our lives to be. My life had been one of trauma, many travels, and living in many different areas. Life as hippies led us to leave our hometown in search of a new foundation for our lives.

One day, shortly after I married William, I told him I wanted to leave our hometown and move to the Northwest. I asked him if he wanted to come with me, and he eagerly agreed. I had a 1960 bright canary-yellow Dodge panel truck with a flat black box that we named Miss Sunburst. We loaded it with just enough necessities to live on a daily basis as we traveled. William built a large, rectangular wooden storage area, painted in Christmas-tree green, and fastened it to the top of the truck with nuts and bolts for our journey. Friends came to our home and painted flowers and other designs on it. After all, we were part of the hippie generation and loved what that represented—peace, love, rock 'n' roll, and an abundance of drugs! I'm not sure why or how our course changed because we had intentions of moving to Oregon. We were told that was where the "long-hairs" were moving now, and that excited us.

My journey on the road to enlightenment began to shape itself the day we left our hometown and ended up moving to a desert region. The morning we left, we drove south thinking we would avoid the snow that had already begun to fall in the Rocky Mountains. Our journey began in the fall of 1971. I had just turned twenty-one years old and was ready for a new beginning.

It was early in the morning as we traveled down the interstate with our dog, Karl. Excitement filled the air, and a wave of joy ran through us, just by being on the road. I felt a freedom I had never felt before. It was a beautiful, cool, sunny day. We hadn't gone far before we saw a hitchhiker—a Native American man who looked around twenty years old—on the side of the road.

"Do you want to pick him up?" I asked.

So we stopped and offered him a ride.

He said, "I am heading south."

I laughed and said, "So are we!"

He had long black hair that hung loosely down his back. His dark-brown eyes seemed focused on his journey. When we invited him to travel with us, he was very appreciative and jumped in. As we talked, the road seemed much more interesting.

The hitchhiker was very friendly and introduced himself. "I am from the Lakota reservation in northern Minnesota and have decided to go on a quest to find myself."

Interestingly enough, that was exactly what my husband and I were doing. I explained, "After William and I were married, I also saw the road and that a spiritual quest was part of my journey. Many long-hairs have moved to Oregon. We're headed there but wanted to avoid the snow in the mountains, so we're taking a southern route."

We smoked marijuana, listened to music, laughed a lot, and shared many stories about our lives as we traveled that day.

Our Lakota friend told us, "Life on the reservation is much different. We do not have the luxuries that are found in other places. I live with three sisters and one brother in a small wooden home that is very simple. My father does odd jobs, and my mother takes care of us kids and does beading work."

I was intrigued by his story. As the hours passed, I talked about my early life.

"I was an only child, but at six months of age, my mother gave me to my grandmother to raise. There was much alcoholism and abuse in my home, and it was safe for me with my grandmother."

William, who had been somewhat quiet, then shared, "I have three brothers and one sister. I am the oldest. My mother died when I was young, and my father was always busy working at the family business, so I did not see much of him."

We talked about experiences we'd had as children and the hope for new life now. Sometimes, we just listened to the silence as we enjoyed each other's energy.

We put on several miles that day, approximately 350, as we talked and got to know each other. We didn't stop to eat because we had food with us. As we entered St. Louis, Missouri, that evening, our friend decided to leave us. We said our goodbyes and went our separate ways. It was sad to part, but there was nowhere for him to sleep. My husband and I decided to stay in St. Louis that night; we parked the panel truck in a residential area of the city and slept there.

The next morning, as we were driving down the entrance ramp to the interstate, we saw our Native American friend again, with his thumb out. We stopped to pick him up, and were very happy to see each other again. We laughed, and I said, "You must have been waiting for us!" Perhaps that was spirit's intent all along. Ironically, he was with us for almost our entire trip, which ended near our new desert home. We eventually parted ways, but I shall not forget him. He was wise yet searching, the same as we were.

William and I camped that evening at the site of an Indian stronghold. It was located in a beautiful mountainous region that was rich with history. An infamous Indian chief was buried in those sacred mountains, which added to the mystery of the area. It was written that he loved these mountains and always considered them his home, even though it was just a winter home for him and his tribe.

As I drifted into slumber that night, my sleep was restless and disturbed. A major battle had been fought during the Indian Wars between the Chiricahua Apache and the US military in the area where we were camped. In my dreams were the spirits of those who fought that battle. I saw Indians running in the tall grasses of the mountains and soldiers trying to kill or capture them. The soldiers were ambushed as they pushed forward, and I could hear yells and screams and saw horses running everywhere.

The next morning, I awakened early and told my husband what I had experienced as I slept. He said he knew that my sleep had been very troubled. I was relieved when we left the region later that morning, but I knew the spirits of all who had been would live on in my memory, as well as the intensity of the fighting and killing that took place in that beautiful, sacred canyon.

We began the journey that morning to where we would unknowingly make our new home—desert surrounded by incredibly beautiful mountains for as far as the eye could see. When we drove, we were never in a hurry because we were on an adventure, and there is no end to a true-life adventure.

That evening, we drove out into the desert. Saguaro cactus dotted the landscape around us in no particular order, so we just drove off into the grassless plain and set up camp. None of this journey had a plan, once we left our Midwestern home, except to stop and view an amazingly breathtaking conglomerate of caverns—as we had traveled west on an exceptionally long stretch of highway, we had seen billboards advertising this mysterious sight.

That night in the desert was very peaceful, much different than the previous night and my restless sleep from having dreams and visions of a battle long ago. When morning arrived, we both felt quite refreshed. We were sitting outside, enjoying our breakfast of fruit and bread, when an elderly Native American man walked up to our campsite. He was of average height, about five foot eight, and was of medium build. His long graying hair was in a braid, and he had a red bandana wrapped around the top of his head. He wore blue jeans and a long-sleeved shirt, buttoned to chest level. On his feet were tattered blue tennis shoes.

He stopped for only a moment and spoke briefly, saying "It's a beautiful day."

We replied, "Good morning. It is a beautiful day."

He then smiled at us, said "I wish you blessings on your journey," and then continued his walk in the desert.

Just for a moment, my husband and I looked down at what we were eating, and when we looked up again, the elderly man had disappeared.

To this day, I don't know if he was a spirit, an angel, or a living man. We both questioned this. I believe he was a spirit.

We drove to the campus of the university in our new city early that afternoon. As we strolled across the campus, we were approached by a young man.

"Are you looking for a job?" he asked. "I'm searching for men who are willing to work at the Convention Center, setting up for a concert tonight."

William eagerly spoke up. "Yeah, I'll help ya out!"

The young man then gave William the address and time to start work. We were both overly excited to have this opportunity, as we had just arrived in the city. Interestingly, as we drove down the interstate that day, I had said, "I would really like to see the Ike and Tina Turner Revue sometime." That evening, I found out that he was setting up chairs in the Convention Center for Ike and Tina Turner! I took him to work, purchased a ticket for myself, and met him inside. This was awesome, and the concert was incredible—another mystical event.

A day later, we decided to have lunch at a local truck stop on the edge of the city and enjoy a cheeseburger and french fries. I jokingly said, "It's a treat to be eating something other than rice, fruit, bread, and peanut butter." Those had been our main staples on this journey. As we ate, we swapped a story or two about our travels with a couple of guys who were sitting at a table across from us. One of the men asked, "Are you planning on staying here, or are you going to continue traveling?"

William said, "We've decided to stay, and I'm going to start looking for a job tomorrow. We also have to find a place to live. We're living out of the back of our panel truck right now."

"My boss is always looking for help," one of the guys said. "He has a landscape business. If you want a job, here's the address. Show up at 5:00 a.m."

William walked out with a job working for a landscaping contractor, driving a tractor that day.

After starting work the next day, his new employer said, "I heard you are looking for a house to rent?"

"Yes, do you know of one?"

"I have a house for rent that you can move into immediately, if you are interested."

We looked at the house after he finished work that day—a one-bedroom house with a kitchen, living room, and bath. It was very clean and neat. The yard was surrounded by a chain-link fence. There was a driveway but no garage. We didn't have any furniture, but it was furnished with twin beds that we pushed together, a kitchen table and chairs, and a stove and refrigerator. It was wonderful, and I loved it. It seemed like everything was working out magically for us.

In mid-November, William's boss invited us to spend our first Thanksgiving in our new location with his family and friends. It was 1971, and we loved our new home and the friends we were making. We also found that our new friends like to drink alcohol quite often and smoke pot. For us, they were great friends because that's what we also did very often.

And that truck stop where we ate—well, I started working as a part-time waitress there. I had never been a waitress, but I thought, *Why not?*

As my quest to find *me* continued, I felt freer every day from the craziness in my family, and life was unfolding in new ways. I had blonde hair that fell to the middle of my back and wore Indian-print clothing that I had made and jeans that I creatively embroidered. My husband was charismatic and quite intelligent and enjoyed conversing. He had long brown hair and wore it in a ponytail. Where we lived was a mecca for long-hairs (hippies) and spirituality. Lots of psychedelic drugs, marijuana, and alcohol. I loved to go to the park when I wasn't working and hang out with musicians and sing and dance. It truly was like the shows you see on TV now about the mid-'60's, and early '70s. We made friends easily and had fun.

As time allowed for exploration and meeting new people, my true spiritual growth began. We frequented a Kundalini Yoga ashram, studied the teachings of Sat Guru Maharaj Ji, chanted and danced with Hare Krishna friends at their temple, and ate *Prasadam* (holy food that is vegetarian and offered to Lord Krishna). My best friend at the time was a Hopi medicine man, whom I loved dearly. We spent many hours together. Sometimes, during the day, we would just walk in the desert, and he would point out nature to me. My eyes saw with him what I did not see on my own.

William and I continued drinking and smoking pot and had started arguing a lot. Day after day, the arguments continued. One early afternoon, I told him I was not feeling well. I was having abdominal cramps and found blood on my pants. I was very weak and asked him to drive me to the hospital, but he refused. I knew I needed medical attention, so I drove myself. I was there for six hours and was told I'd had a miscarriage. I then had to drive myself back home. My sadness and feeling alone was overwhelming. I had no one with whom to share my heartbreak, as my husband did not want to hear about it.

Not long after this, we moved in with one of the men William worked with. We rented a very nice two-bedroom home, with a sunny sitting room off the living room, a big kitchen, bathroom, and sunporch on the back of the house. We had a lovely yard with a large orange tree in the center of it, as well as a garage. I started working again for a short time, and the arguing decreased.

Unbeknownst to me, I was about to embark upon another adventure. This time, it was the privilege of experiencing life in a tepee camp in the mountains near Mexico. Two friends of mine from the Midwest lived in a tepee there and invited me to visit—we had met up again, surprisingly, at a food co-op where I was working. It was great seeing them, and I made it my quest to visit their camp. I talked to William about this adventure.

"Go ahead and do it," he said. "I think it would be great."

Our housemate's girlfriend went with me, and William and our housemate stayed home and worked.

We drove there in a jeep. Before ascending up the mountains, we came to an abandoned gold and silver mining town, just north of the Mexican border. Some wealthy people back East had hired a group of long-hairs to care for the area. A small pond was at this level, and those who lived in the mountains would come down periodically to bathe in it and make candles in the sand.

There were two tepee camps, an upper and a lower camp, which were located in different areas in the mountains. The only way to get to them was by climbing the long, difficult mountainous terrain or by jeep, over large rocks and around jagged boulders.

The tepees were of different sizes. In one very large tepee was a family—a mother, father, and eight children. Life was very simple, and you worked hard for what you needed; that is, gardening, sharing an outdoor oven, and cooking with others. This lifestyle was quite freeing from the events in our country at the time, with civil rights unrest and the Vietnam War in full scale.

After I'd returned home from my excursion to the tepee camp, my mother and brother came to visit for a couple of days over Easter. Prior to that, William had talked about going on a trip with another long-hair and a young woman in a big Crown Coach bus and making jewelry and lamps. I didn't want to do that; it didn't feel right to me. I don't think I trusted them, so I said, "I don't feel good about this. I'm not going to join you." I tried to talk him into staying home, but he wanted to go. He left on the same day my mother and brother left. I felt really alone and didn't know what I was going to do. I was on yet another journey by myself.

About two weeks later, I decided to drive out to meet my husband at a wharf on the West Coast—that's where he told me they were headed. I packed up my yellow-and-black panel truck, along with my dog. All I knew was that I was heading to the Coast to find him. But as fate would have it, many adventures were to be had on that journey.

As I was driving down the road, feeling kind of like a Jack Kerouac-type traveler, I started to get hungry. Lo and behold, just ahead was a root beer drive-in, and that tripped the trigger of my taste buds, so I pulled in. A carhop came to my truck window, and I said, "I'd like to order a hot dog with ketchup and mustard." When it arrived, I thought, *This hot dog looks a little gray, but I'm hungry.* I gobbled it down happily with my frosty mug of root beer. Fed and feeling good, I continued on my journey.

I never knew how far I was going to drive; I just headed on down the road. Before long, I saw a hitchhiker. Back in those days, hitchhikers were pretty safe; he was a long-hair, and I needed the conversation. (My dog was an excellent listener but short on conversation!)

My new acquaintance jumped in, but my extremely protective dog was not welcoming to this stranger. Finally, he settled down; he stopped barking and trying to sit on the seat where the hitchhiker was sitting. My dog, a German shepherd/collie mix, weighed about sixty pounds. He diligently kept his eye on our new companion.

We talked and laughed as I drove down the highway. Everything was going well—until I suddenly became extremely sick. I was nauseated and had to make a stop at an upcoming roadside bar and grill. The restrooms were out behind this establishment, and I made a beeline for them. The hitchhiker went into the bar and grill while I was in the restroom, vomiting and having diarrhea. I couldn't even tell him what was happening. Eventually, he came to check on me

"I'm very sick," I muttered.

"Why don't you try to get back in the truck?" he said.

Barely able to talk, I replied, "I don't know if I can."

"Just try."

I was in that restroom for what seemed like hours. Finally, I was able to get back to the truck. "Can you drive?" I asked him

"Yes," he said, but he looked worried.

We continued down the road. He knew where I was going, which was good because I couldn't say much at all; I just lay there in the back of the panel truck, feeling sick. I can't remember his name now, but he was a godsend for me. As we traveled on, I started feeling worse and, in a very weak voice, I said, "Please check into the nearest hotel or motel, whatever you can find quickly. I am very sick."

He found a hotel in a very small town and unloaded me, checked us in, and got me up to the room. He then left the room.

I lay in bed but knew I had to get to the bathroom and ended up crawling there. When he came back to check on me, I was in very serious condition. He came into the bathroom and said, "Oh my God!" He left the room and brought the manager back with him.

I don't remember the ambulance coming; I was unconscious at that time. I do remember being on a gurney in what I assumed was a hospital. My soul had left my body, and my spirit was hovering above, looking down at my body. There were people in white—doctors and nurses—attempting to talk to me. They kept saying, "What is your name?" I kept telling them, but they could not hear me. It was my spirit that was trying to communicate with them. I heard them say, "We are losing her," and—silence.

I woke up in an unfamiliar hospital in San Jose, California, the following day. My nurse said, "You had food poisoning and had to be transferred here because the other hospital was not equipped to keep you alive." I was still sick when she gave me that news; I just slept. As the days went by, wellness started taking over my body, and my strength returned. I had a wonderful roommate, with whom I quickly became friends. She lived in the region.

The orderly who took care of me said, "Your dog is in a dog pound. You can pick him up when you're discharged." I was relieved to hear that and could only imagine what had to be done to get him out of that truck. He also said, "Your truck is in a police compound. You can also pick that up after discharge from the hospital."

I felt so fortunate to have this cared for. "What about the hitchhiker?" I asked.

No one had any information about him. I'd spent several hours with a man whose name I did not remember but who had saved my life.

The orderly assigned to my room was a very warm and friendly young man. He lived in a small town several miles from the hospital, up in the forest area. He had graciously taken my clothes home and washed them, as they were covered in vomit and feces from the food poisoning. He returned them, fresh and clean, for my discharge. He gave me his address and phone number and compassionately said, "If you have the time, I would like you to visit me."

I thanked him for everything and happily said, "I will try to do so."

My hospital roommate, Sherry, was discharged a day earlier than I was. We came to know each other, as we spent hours talking during my five-day hospital stay.

Sherry offered to pick me up when I was discharged. "I'd like to invite you to stay at my house for a couple of days until you have more strength," she said. I happily agreed.

Being in the company of this young woman was yet another adventure. Her boyfriend worked on the campus of a large university in California. The killings of the students at Kent State were still fresh in America's minds and protesting against the Vietnam War was at its peak.

Sherry's boyfriend asked us to visit him at the campus one particular afternoon. As we were standing there talking, loud noises erupted across the street. I turned and saw the National Guard charging toward a building on the corner adjacent to us and rushing in. Students were screaming and jumping from second- and third-story windows. Sherry's boyfriend grabbed our hands, and we started running as fast as we could, away from the area. We just kept running until we were far away from the invasion. I was breathless and extremely frightened.

Sherry quickly said, "We are getting out of here." We jumped in her car and drove off. I have no idea what happened after we left, but I hope no one died that day. Sherry and I were both numb and in shock. I told her, "I think it's time for me to continue my journey." She understood.

She drove me to the police station compound, and I picked up my truck and then drove to pick up my dog. I thanked them all for helping me when I was so sick. My poor dog was so happy to see me that he almost knocked me over with excitement. I was not charged for any of the services by the police department. More blessings.

After a week or so, I decided to visit the dear orderly who had helped me so graciously. He was wonderfully welcoming; he lived in a yoga ashram. We talked about my journey and my spiritual quest. He said, "I too am on a spiritual quest. Yoga has opened me to myself."

I spent the day with him and his friend. It was a beautifully enlightening visit.

My journey continued as I drove to the Coast and began my search at the wharf, but there was no William to be found. I asked people, "Have you seen a big Crown Coach or anyone making or selling jewelry or lamps in this area?" No one had. I finally gave up my search. Instead, I spent time visiting old friends, making new friends, eating only dates—because I was afraid to eat anything else—and making my way down the coastal highway, just me and my dog. Eventually, after many excursions along the way, I began my long trek back to my desert haven.

I had to travel many miles again across the great desert. This area was all sand and sand dunes, with sporadic growths of creosote bush and bur sage. It was extremely hot, and it was not uncommon to see an overheated vehicle pulled over on the side of the road.

People would hang bags of water on the side of their vehicles' mirrors in case the vehicle overheated. I didn't have one but often saw them on other cars. I went through that area twice with a prayer that my truck would not overheat.

I returned safely home. Our housemate no longer lived there, however, so I had to find a place to stay that night. I spoke with a friend of mine who was bartending. "I have nowhere to live and am wondering if I could stay at your house tonight?"

He was most accommodating, and I was thrilled! The following day, I found my tribe of friends and moved in with them. I felt very alone and wasn't sure what I was going to do. I had some money, as living simply was not costly. I wasn't charged any rent where I stayed; I think my friends felt sorry for me. I usually went to the park during the day and listened to music or walked in the desert with my Hopi friend. I didn't make plans; I mostly lived from day to day. I knew so many people, and this was my home now.

One morning a few months later, to my astonishment, I looked out the front door and saw William walking up the sidewalk. One of the guys he had worked with told him where I was living, and he found me. He said he'd been kicked off the bus and had hitchhiked back here. We talked about what had happened since we'd last seen each other, including my sickness.

"There was a four-point bulletin out for you in the state of California," I said. "You could not be found."

"Yeah, we decided to go to Boulder instead."

I was amazed that he had not been in contact with me in all that time, and everything that had gone on with me, including my almost dying from food poisoning, seemed to be no big deal. He was able to go back to work for the same landscaping business, and we moved into a house with one of his coworkers. It was as if all that had happened was just a blip in time.

We continued our spiritual practices, as well as our drug and alcohol use. My Hopi friend then told me of my pregnancy. I was surprised and excited. I stopped drinking, but there was no evidence at that time that marijuana use was a danger to a fetus, so I continued to smoke pot.

I had never been across the Mexican border, so one afternoon William, our roommate, and I went on a several-hours excursion to Mexico. I developed hepatitis A from the drinking water. I'd been very thirsty and drank from a fountain on the outside of an old cement-block building. At that time, I did not know that I shouldn't drink the water in Mexico.

I became very sick. I had no appetite and could not keep down any food. My nourishment was a liquid diet of red clover–leaf tea. William had learned that this tea was good medicine for my illness. I became quite thin; I spent the first three months of pregnancy feeling extremely ill. Doctors could do nothing for me, but thankfully, with time, I eventually recovered. My baby was not harmed; that had been my biggest fear.

Three months later, William and I talked about the idea of moving back to the Midwest, where our families were. This became our next adventure. We thought we would have help if we needed it, and our baby could get to know his family. That seemed to be the avenue to pursue, so we did. We returned that fall after being gone for a year and a half.

William went to work for the family business, which led to much stress for him. We rented a farmhouse for several months and had two housemates. After Daniel's birth, when I was twenty-two years old, life became more intense. The use of alcohol, marijuana, and LSD became more prevalent, especially marijuana on a daily basis. Daniel had colic, so we barely slept. William was becoming angrier, and I didn't know how to handle the situation. I saw the change in him. "Every time you do LSD you become a different person," I told him.

"You don't know what the hell you are talking about," he snarled.

He was an avid reader and seemed to take on the characteristics of the main character in the book he was reading. My senses kept me on guard whenever I was around him.

I breastfed Daniel when he was born and felt such a loving bond with him. When we were alone, I would turn on music, hold him in my arms, and dance around the living room. He really enjoyed this. I would say, "Does Mommy's Dumples like this?" He would smile; we had our own peaceful moments.

As the arguing became more intense, the stress of our fighting was too hard on me. I cried to my doctor, "I don't know what is happening. Daniel seems to be hungry all the time, but he isn't getting the nourishment from me that he needs."

"I'm sorry, but your breast milk is drying up, most likely from the stress," the doctor said. "I think you will have to start giving him formula."

My heart was broken, and I became angrier at William. When I returned home from the doctor's, I said, "I have to start buying formula because my breast milk is drying up."

He just said, "Well, you better do it, then."

Shortly after this, William was arrested for growing marijuana. He served jail time but only on weekends, under the Huber Law. Our marriage was suffering, and he had become physically abusive. We moved back into town because I didn't want to be stranded in the country with no vehicle during the winter months. We rented a big three-bedroom house with a living room, dining room, bath, kitchen, fenced-in yard, and garage. I really liked this new home. I felt safer in town, but William's anger kept escalating.

I could tell the mood he was in when he walked up the sidewalk to the house after work. I lived in fear most of the time. Now, I was the one with bruises—bruises from his hands on my wrists, bruises on my breasts and upper arms. I kept thinking, *How did I get here? Why is my life like this?* I started going out to bars with my girlfriends at night and drinking heavily, besides smoking marijuana and doing LSD. I took Daniel to my mother's to stay overnight when I did LSD because I knew I couldn't care for him during those times. My drinking escalated, my marriage had already fallen apart, and I was trying to protect myself and Daniel from William.

One day, Daniel and I had not been able to get home by the time William arrived for lunch, and he was angry that I was not there. It was winter, and a recent snowstorm had left the streets difficult to navigate due to ice layered under the snow. I attempted to drive the truck up a hill that led to our home but couldn't make it up the hill. Finally, a man came along and was able to get the truck turned around so I could take another route. When I walked in with my son, I saw that all of my clothes and Daniel's clothes were thrown all over the living floor.

"Get out!" William shouted.

I started crying. "Why have you done this?"

"Get the fuck out!"

I pleaded with him to stop, but he pushed me, and I fell against the wall. My son was crying, and William was out of control with anger. I kept begging him, "Please don't do this. Please stop doing this!"

Finally, it was like something snapped inside of him, and he stopped. He grabbed his jacket and left. I put all of our clothes back in the drawers and closets, and when he arrived home from work, he was kind, as if nothing had happened earlier that day.

Shortly after that scene, we learned that the house we were renting was going to be sold. We had the option to buy, but we chose not to. We then moved to another house in the country. I did not like it there; I felt we were too far away from people. William's brother and one of William's friends moved in with us. One night, when William was drunk and high on LSD, we had a big fight. I ran out the door with my son and jumped in the car and drove to town.

The next day, I left my son at my mom's and went back out to our house. All of my possessions had been destroyed. The inside of the refrigerator was busted in pieces. My toaster oven was bent in half, my bed frame was partially hanging out of the upstairs window, and things were strewn all over. I grabbed two bags of clothing for my son, and I and left. I called the sheriff, and he went out there. William's friend had destroyed everything, and I said, "Enough is enough." I never went back again. I knew then that this behavior was getting much too dangerous and that I had to do something to keep Daniel and myself safe.

I moved Daniel and me into a house in our hometown. I divorced William when I was twenty-five and started feeling some peace again. Still, there were problems with the formula Daniel was drinking, and he was in and out of the hospital due to vomiting and diarrhea in those first two years. I read so much information on his condition and finally came to my own conclusion; I approached his doctor and said, point-blank, "Did you ever think that he might be allergic to dairy products?"

The doctor shook his head. "No, I never thought of that. Maybe that's the problem."

Daniel was in the hospital at the time, so the doctor scheduled an exploratory surgery to see if there was an internal problem causing blood in his urine, vomiting, and diarrhea.

I agreed because I was unsure of what to do. At 5:00 a.m., the pastor from the church I was affiliated with came to the hospital and prayed over Daniel. Before the surgery, tests were taken. The concern of blood in his urine, vomiting, and diarrhea were gone.

I told the doctor, "A miracle has happened."

My two-year-old son was then discharged, and I took him home. I experimented with a variety of milks—goat's milk, soy milk, and powdered milk; powdered milk was the answer. Daniel had no more digestive issues. He was on a dairy-free and sugar-free diet. During all of this and during Daniel's hospitalizations, William was not in the picture.

It had been a difficult marriage, filled with adventure and abuse. The strong point of the relationship was our ability to communicate with each other to make the adventures fun and interesting. Both of us had experienced much strife in our families of origin. We didn't know how to be married, but we tried for as long as we could. I never doubted the love that was there; it just wasn't our time. His pain came out as physical anger with me.

One evening, after we had been divorced for a year or so, I overheard a conversation he was having with a friend of his, and I was brought to tears. He looked intently at his friend and said, "One thing I would like to say about Celeste is that she taught me how to laugh, and she taught me how to cry."

Thereafter, my thoughts of him were awakened, and I saw the little boy whose mother had died from cancer when he was not yet a teenager. He'd kept all that sadness locked inside. He truly could not cry a tear when I first came to know him, and I will never forget the setting or the look on his face when his first tear came.

After our divorce, he asked me if I would like to work for their family business. They needed a bookkeeper, and I agreed. Our working together was sometimes challenging. The business paid for day care for Daniel and provided benefits, such as being able to take time off if my son was ill.

At times, the past would rear its ugly head again, and my now ex-husband would yell and argue and demonstrate his abusive nature. One day, he came through the door at work, angry, and pushed me up against the filing cabinets.

I screamed, "What's wrong with you? Leave me alone!" I grabbed my purse and ran out the door.

Later, his father came to see me, and I told him what it had been like to work with William.

After much conversation, he said, "I promise that if you come back to work, I will make sure this never happens again. Take a month to think about it, and then let me know."

After a month, I agreed to come back to work. There were no more problems after that.

Living on my own with Daniel was very freeing. No more fighting, no more abuse—at least, not from William. Slowly, my mother was exerting more of her dominance in my life with Daniel. When I wanted to go out with friends, my mother would babysit. I was still drinking and drugging almost daily; I smoked marijuana every day but could not drink daily because it made me sick. My mother started making comments about my life, and Daniel heard her condescending remarks to me.

I was not a strong person when it came to her verbal abuse. I didn't have the skills yet to stand up to her. I still had my demons from the abusive life I had with her that kept me stuck. I was a victim and had not yet learned how to release myself from her power over me. There were many arguments, which she won. My escape was through alcohol and drugs. In reality, I never escaped; the chemicals just kept me numb. The awakening door of my spirituality had been closed, and my addiction was alive and taking over my life.

One evening, I went to a park to listen to a band playing in one of the pavilions. I was standing amid a large crowd of people, dancing in place. Standing next to me was a rather tall man with long black hair and a black goatee; he was wearing a black leather jacket. We smiled at each other.

"Hi, I'm Celeste," I said.

"I'm Ben," he replied. "Are you from here?"

I told him I was. We danced and drank beer and smoked pot. At the end of the evening, we hugged each other, and he jumped on his Harley-Davidson motorcycle and drove off. I was smitten by his playfulness and conversation. At age twenty-seven, I still experienced the uncontrollable wrath of my mother's character disorder and untreated alcoholism, and I saw this man as my knight on his steel horse.

As time went on, Ben and I started spending time together and decided to cohabitate. He seemed to be very attentive, and we got along well together. He had a good job and was committed to our relationship. Daniel liked him, and life took the form of a family. One day, he teasingly asked, "What was it about me that made you really like me?"

I laughed. "The day you stood in the doorway when you were leaving, threw your cap up in the air, and it came back down and landed on your head!" We both laughed, but seriously, I was impressed.

One year later, in 1979, I married Ben. He was also chemically dependent, although initially, I didn't know that. After a year of marriage, it became clear. I knew I had a problem but was still continuing to use chemicals, and we drank and used drugs together. Ben became verbally abusive to Daniel around that time. It began subtly and slowly at first, by ordering him around. Then, he started handling him roughly and swearing at him. He frequently said, "You little son of a bitch," when he ordered him to do something.

I told him repeatedly, "Stop treating my son like that," but he wouldn't stop." He would usually just grab a beer and walk away.

After two years of marriage, Ben and I were on his Harley-Davidson, under the extreme influence of alcohol and marijuana, and he drove off a curve. We'd been at a party all afternoon and evening. I was very intoxicated and said I wanted to leave. He agreed and we drove off on his bike—and seven miles into the ride, he missed the curve.

I barely remember being on the bike. I kept going in and out of being in a blackout, but I do remember lying on the ground and feeling pain in my jaw, believing it was broken. Ben asked, "Can you get up?"

I crawled to my feet, with his help. He stood the bike up, and we both got back on it. I then realized we were in a ditch, and he was driving up to the road. When we got to the road, the bike went down again on the big yellow sign that we apparently had knocked down when he drove off the road. I was in so much pain, crying and holding my jaw. He picked the bike up again, and we rode it back to the party.

I was taken to the hospital in someone's car, about thirty-five miles away. We got a sheriff's escort after being stopped for speeding on the highway. The driver of the car explained to the sheriff, "I'm taking this woman to the hospital. There was a motorcycle accident."

I was drunk, stoned, hurt, and scared.

At the hospital, the nurses asked, "Have you taken any drugs tonight?" I said no, even though I had been smoking marijuana all day, along with the alcohol consumption. I was afraid to tell them the truth because I thought I would be sent to jail.

The next day, Ben and his friend went back to the farm where the party had been to pick up his motorcycle, but it was so badly damaged, he couldn't ride it. He had to come back home and get his pickup truck to haul his motorcycle home. The bike had rebar iron wrapped around the back brake, and the clutch handle was broken off. Although it was impossible to ride the bike, he had driven us back to the party on it so that I could be transported to the hospital by car. All I could think of was that the angels brought us back to the party on that bike.

Due to the lower-back injuries I suffered in the accident, I began treatments with a chiropractor. I was walking only when necessary because the back pain had increased significantly. I was under my doctor's care, but he wasn't able to help much, except with prescribing medications. The injuries from the accident included temporomandibular joint dislocation (TMJ) of my jaw, three crushed discs in my lumbar region, and an injured left knee. I had to have ultrasound on my jaw several times because it was dislocated so badly, and that was the only way to get my jaw in alignment again.

I was on a steady diet of pain pills and muscle relaxants. Ben experienced much remorse over my condition after the accident. One day, he took my hands and said, "I am so sorry for what has happened to you." He had tears in his eyes.

"I am the one who chose to get on the bike that night," I said. "You didn't make me."

"But I should have known better than to let you get on the bike. Before we went off the curve, I'd turned my head to see if you were OK, and I didn't see the curve coming up in the dark."

As the days went by, the pain felt like thousands of electrical shocks moving up and down my spine. My doctor recommended a wheelchair because of the pain. Standing up was virtually impossible without help. Sometimes, I would just sit in the wheelchair or lie in my bed and cry. I didn't know what to do, and no one seemed to want to help me. I knew I should have back surgery. I went to the most prestigious medical centers, but no one wanted to operate. The doctors said, "It's a very delicate surgery, and unless you come crawling in, we won't do surgery."

My girlfriend had accompanied me to the doctor that day. I told her, "The doctor won't operate. He said it's too dangerous."

"Oh, Celeste," she said, "I'm so sorry."

I cried all the way home; I don't think I ever went through a day without crying. I spent almost four years in a wheelchair and in and out of the hospital frequently, due to the excruciating pain in my back.

One of the medical centers wanted me to try a body cast to see if it would help. I lay on a table in the clinic and was wrapped from behind, starting at my neck, all the way down past my lower back. On the front of me, the wrappings started under my breasts and went down to my pubic bone. The doctor said, "Wear this cast for a month. Hopefully, it will help with your pain."

Cleaning up was really a fiasco. When I showered, Ben placed a rain poncho over my cast and used a shower hose to wash my hair and legs. I developed some very ingenious methods for my daily self-care.

My days consisted of taking pain pills and muscle relaxants and smoking marijuana. It was 1981, and I lived in an altered reality, surrounded by fear, anxiety, and pain.

After the motorcycle accident, Ben often yelled at Daniel and sent him to his room or wouldn't allow him to do things that were noisy. I was always saying, "Stop yelling at him. He is a child!" I was in protective mode with my son all the time. I didn't want him to be alone with Ben.

Due to my very poor physical health from the accident, I thought if I kept Daniel away from Ben as much as I could, at least on weekends, it would be better for him. The only thing I knew to do at the time was to ask my mother to take care of him at least once a week. She never wanted to care for him any longer than one day and evening, but any time for him to get away from Ben was good.

Ben kept drinking every day. He woke up in the morning, and the first thing he did was open a can of beer. This would go on until bedtime.

Sadly, the abuse escalated with Daniel. During one of my hospitalizations, Ben became angry because my then-nine-year-old son had not put his laundry away. Daniel and his friend were going to a movie that day. As Ben told me the story about the laundry, he became angrier, and suddenly, he grabbed Daniel by the collar of his jacket and threw him across the room. He fell to the floor behind a chair in the corner of the hospital room.

I screamed, "Get out! Get out of here right now!"

I was in the hospital because of the horrible pain I was experiencing and couldn't walk, but when that happened, I jumped out of bed, ran to the corner, pulled away the chair, and picked up my little son, who was stunned and crying. His neck was bleeding from being cut by the zipper on his jacket.

My mother and the pastor from the church I attended had come to visit and witnessed this abuse; they sat there silently. After I told Ben to leave my hospital room, I asked my mother to take Daniel home with her.

Later that evening, she called me. "You better call Ben and tell him you are sorry for kicking him out of your hospital room because you won't have anywhere to go. There's no one who will take care of you."

Daniel and I had to return home to Ben. I prayed and prayed that God would make me better so we could leave there. I was always guarded and extremely protective of Daniel. Fear ran through my body like the blood flowing through my veins. My adrenaline surged whenever Ben was home. One Saturday afternoon, I heard Ben's voice thundering from the living room through the hallway and into the kitchen, where I was sitting.

"Get upstairs," he shouted, "and stay there until I tell you to come down!"

Immediately, my body tensed up and my shoulders tightened. I yelled, "Ben, would you come in here right now?" When he walked in, I said, "If you ever touch my son again, I will kill you."

He stood there, dazed. He knew I was serious. Ben walked out of the kitchen and out the door. He never raised his voice or threatened Daniel again.

One morning, about three months later, I woke up feeling much lighter. The pain had decreased, and I had hope. I felt that God was answering my prayers. I decided it was time to move. I called a realtor in town; he said that he had a two-bedroom house for rent. I drove into town and looked at the house, then rented it, and when Ben was at work two days later, I packed some of our belongings and moved that day. Daniel was confused but trusted me. We moved to our new home and started building a new life. God knew I needed to protect my son, and God blessed the pathway for us.

Daniel was ten years old when we left that marriage. Two years later, I was still having problems with my back, but it wasn't as severe as when I lived with Ben. I believe that the daily stress exacerbated the pain. My chiropractor provided an avenue for me to have lumbar surgery, and in 1984, I came through a very difficult surgery and was able to walk. It was a prayer answered.

My addiction to drugs and alcohol had become overwhelming, and the addition of pain pills and muscle relaxants added to the cocktail of paranoia, fear, and more insecurity than ever. My escape from life had begun when I started drinking and then using drugs of all varieties at an early age. I had my first half can of beer at thirteen years of age, while at a high school party; now, my life was completely out of control.

As time went on, I saw myself as a garbage can for drugs but always drew the line at heroin or using any drug intravenously. I was a daily marijuana smoker for almost two decades but somehow kept my desire to learn. My illusory existence of chemical use kept me alive.

I was afraid to be alone when Daniel was away for an evening or, worse yet, when he would go to camp for a few weeks in the summer. I had parties after the bars closed at night so I wouldn't have to be alone. I had no direction in life, even though I was now back in school, working on my undergraduate degree. Vocational rehabilitation had been working with me since having back surgery, and Daniel and I lived on Social Security disability because I'd been 100 percent disabled from the motorcycle accident. Deep down inside, I begged myself to have a better life, but I just kept using chemicals.

Attending college was a continuing dream, but the first year in school as a nontraditional student while using chemicals was quite challenging for me. The week of finals was a blur. On the evening I was to take my abnormal psychology final, I spent the day drinking and smoking marijuana. I am still amazed that the instructor allowed me into the classroom. I can only imagine how I smelled to those around me. I was ashamed of my behavior at the time, but it was who I was. When grades were posted, I saw that I'd received a B on the final.

I doubted myself often and my ability to stay focused. Suicide had been weighing heavily on my mind. The chemical use gave me no reprieve, and I felt as if I was being swallowed by my own dark side. I had a meeting with an attorney to draw up a will to ensure all that I owned would be secured by my son. That was the first step in my suicide plan. I was also contemplating where Daniel would be when I committed this act against myself so that he wouldn't find me. When I think about that now, I can only remember the dark despair I was experiencing as my life crumbled, and suicide seemed the only way out.

Early one evening, as I sat in my living room, I heard a knock on the door. Daniel raced to the door to see who it was. There stood my college professor and a handful of classmates, holding large brown-paper bags full of groceries, laundry soap, and paper products. I was stunned by what I saw. They set the bags on my dining room table and said, "We know things have been difficult for you, and we thought these groceries might help."

Tears welled up in my eyes as I thanked them profusely for their help. As my classmates started to leave, my instructor handed me an envelope, hugged me, and then walked out the door. I was crying now, and Daniel was busily looking through the bags of groceries. He was thirteen years old and didn't grasp what was happening, but I certainly did.

In my brokenness, I opened the envelope. Inside was a note that read, "I usually donate money each year to a necessary cause. This year, I thought that you needed it more." Enclosed was fifty dollars. I could barely breathe between my tears. I could only think, *I can't believe that someone loves me this much.* At the time, we barely had any food to eat, and I had spent a few thousand dollars in a very short time on my addiction. My outlook on life was quite bleak. Now, with a table full of food and supplies and a gift of money in my hand, I knew something had to change, although I wasn't aware of how that would happen. Those beautiful earth angels had given me a gift that went beyond material; it knocked at the door of my heart and on the door of reason.

Now, after talking with my spirit mentor about this incident, I learned that all of what I have experienced has been on my blueprint for this life. This being the journey and the path.

Shortly after this incident, I made plans to go out with my best girlfriend from school. She was not aware of my chemical dependency, and I ended up driving us home while in a blackout that evening. The next morning, I awoke on my living room couch, fully dressed—and with the front door wide open. I got up to see if my car was parked in the driveway and then came back inside. I fell to my knees on the living room floor, crying, and asked God to come into my life and help me because I could not help myself.

My phone rang then; it was my girlfriend. She heard the distress in my voice, but I couldn't express what was happening to me. She said, "Celeste, I want to ask you a question. Why do you drink so much?"

I choked on my words and clumsily answered, "Because I don't like who I am. When I'm drunk, I am not afraid, and I can be anyone I want to be!"

"My husband is an alcoholic," she said. "I will help you."

I went to my first AA meeting on June 23, 1986, and declared my addiction to all who were present at that meeting. Many people I'd known in my drinking and drugging life were there and welcomed me with open arms.

That was my sobriety date, and I now have thirty-five years of freedom from drugs and alcohol, by God's grace.

In time, I came to understand more about my addiction. What has stuck with me the most about my idea that suicide was the way out is this: Many who commit suicide do not want their lives to be over; rather, it is a homicide against the part of who they are that contains the pain. They just want the pain to end.

I became very focused on recovery, and my second year of college was wonderful. I was an officer in Phi Theta Kappa (National Honor Society), a Student Senate senator, and I worked on the Student Activities Committee. I loved being a student again, and that college year was fun and full of adventure, but I still was experiencing difficulty with back pain.

That holiday season, my son and I attended the Christmas Eve service at church. The church was full of people, and as we sat in our pew, the pastor announced there were five faith healers in the congregation that evening.

"If anyone wants healing after the service," he said, "come down and kneel at the altar.

Daniel and I got up and started walking toward the end of our pew, but he stopped and said, "Mom, what are you going to do?"

I looked at him. "I don't know." Then, without hesitation, I walked down to the altar and kneeled.

When the faith healers walked up to me, one asked, "What can we help you with?"

Tears already had formed in my eyes as I looked up and spoke in a voice I barely recognized. "I was in a motorcycle accident that resulted in a lumbar fusion, and I still have quite a bit of pain in my back. I'm also six months in recovery from drugs and alcohol." I hadn't planned on telling them about my recovery; it just seemed to flow out of my mouth.

They spoke in tongues over me and anointed me with oil. When they laid hands on me, everything blacked out. What happened during that time, however, was the feeling of a lightning bolt going from the top of my head, down my spine, and out the end of my tailbone. When I came to and opened my eyes, I was standing in the middle of a group of women from my church, and I was breathing in pure, fresh air. I later came to know that I was breathing in the Holy Spirit.

Daniel and I went home that night, and I was able to sit with him on the couch for the first time in five years, due to my back injury. Previously, I had only been able to sit on hard straight chairs. We both cried. I asked him what he'd seen at church.

"It looked like your head was being torn off," he said.

I'm not sure what he saw, but Daniel was convinced he saw a miracle that night. We were so grateful and happy that Christmas Eve. I knew once more that God had favor with me.

For the first year after I went into recovery from my addictions, my mother would not talk to me. I had stepped out of the family disease and was not accepted. She would come to my home and visit with Daniel but not speak to me, even though we were in the same room. My son never asked why my mother treated me the way she did. In fact, he never said anything about her condescending behavior. He had seen her verbally abuse me and had been subjected to it himself, so he quietly accepted the interactions as normal. It was heartbreaking, but I was too insecure in my awareness of myself to handle the situation maturely. If I had been more secure, Daniel would have been spared the transgressions he experienced by having her in his life.

Out of necessity, I built a camaraderie with fellow recovering addicts. Their loving attention kept me sober until I could learn to love myself, and then they continued to love me more.

My young teenage son was very supportive of my new journey. He was raised in my recovery as I attended an abundance of twelve-step meetings and gatherings of other fellow recovering friends. Daniel and I learned new ways of fulfilling our lives through camping trips, potluck dinners, and movie nights, to name a few. Others also had children, and we all became great friends. Every child was affected severely by alcohol and other addictions, so it was extremely beneficial for the children to know they were not alone in living with chemically dependent families.

I completed my bachelor's degree in social work in 1989. Life was going much better. My back healed, I was three years in recovery, and my son was sixteen—and then the phone call came.

In 1990, through the help and dedication of one earth angel who worked as a social worker for the adoption agency that had placed my children, I found both Sean and Christian. The laws had changed, and the records could be opened so that children who had been placed for adoption could choose to have contact with their birth mothers, if so inclined.

The social worker explained to me that my first son, Sean, wanted to have contact. I was happy, scared, excited, and extremely nervous. We had many phone conversations on how this connection would unfold.

I had never told Daniel about his brothers. I had thought it best not to open my deep wounds from the past. Every day, I thought about my first two sons, but they were part of me that I kept buried from the rest of the world. Now, I was facing what scared me the most at the time, and that was to tell Daniel the story of many years past, when his mother was only as old as he was then.

Daniel and I sat down one evening, and I told him about his brothers. Initially, he was very excited, but then he became angry because I'd kept it from him. He didn't understand because he had no reference point, but it was far from peaceful in our home.

As conversations continued with the social worker, I learned that my second son's adoptive parents had requested my and his father's medical history, if I had that information. I completed quite an extensive medical history and returned it to her.

My first son, Sean, was just finishing college at the time. We wrote letters to each other and finally met about a year later. When I saw him, I saw me. We embraced our reconnection with each other and, along with Daniel, spent ten years together attempting to build a family. Daniel then began heavily using drugs and alcohol. Two years later, he was admitted to a treatment center for substance abuse.

Sean did the best he could with the situation. When he was visiting one day, he said, "I will never have with you what Daniel has."

I was so surprised to hear that and lovingly said, "But we now have what we are building, and I am so blessed to have that with you."

We did many things together at my house, at his house, and with my mom and grandma—fun little adventures—but I could always tell something was not quite right.

During a phone call one day, he said, "I never told my adoptive mother about you." She had died from alcoholism and came to him in a dream one night. "She told me to never forget about her, that she was my mom." After that, I felt a distance each time we spoke.

One day he called and said, "Renae is pregnant." Renae was his girlfriend.

"What are you going to do with this?" I asked.

His answer was stark to my ears. "I'm sure you're worried I might turn out like you did when you were pregnant with me."

"You have a choice in this," I said.

"We are going to be married after our child is born."

I felt relief rush through my body and told him, "You are wise. I love you."

Daniel was so excited.

After the birth of Sean's son, I had planned to visit them in the hospital, along with Daniel.

Sean called the night before my visit, however, and said, "I don't want you to come to the hospital. I don't know if I want you to be part of my son's life."

I was devastated, and so was Daniel.

We spent about forty-five minutes on the phone before we hung up, both of us crying and trying to reason this decision. There was no resolution.

Today, I write to him two to three times a year and let him know how I am and that I love him. The loss remains tucked away in a corner of my heart.

Before the birth of his child, Sean's biological father was able to meet him. He still lives overseas, and after his college years, he developed a wine college; this became his lifelong profession. This year on Valentine's Day, fifty-four years later, I still got a letter that asked if I would be his valentine. We always have had special care for each other; time does not erase the significance of this aged relationship and the birth of our child.

Circumstances with my second son, Christian, were much different. He chose not to meet me. His life was well adjusted, and he wanted to leave it as it was. My heart overflows with love for his adoptive mother, who stepped forward, wrote beautiful letters to me about him, and sent pictures of him as he was growing up. He was in college at that time, a business major. She said she had tried to encourage him to meet me, but he chose not to. His adoptive mother wrote, "He is happy, plays guitar, and likes to hunt." She also thanked me in one of her letters for having the strength to place him for adoption. She wrote, "It must have been the hardest thing you've ever had to do."

I cried when I read these words and thought, *If only you knew.*

Christian felt peace with his adoptive family, who had loved him for so many years, and that brought peace to me.

I told his biological father about the letters and showed him the pictures of our son. He is an author and musician and has written several books of prose, poetry, and stories of past years. He gave me a series of books to give to Christian, if our paths bring us back to each other one more time.

Daniel wears the scar of having one brother who was in his life for only a few years and another he never met. When he is angry, it spews from his mouth like venom. He has no idea what it has been like for me with these great losses. My scars lie deep within my heart. My body remembers what it was to have been pregnant with them and then to release them.

Daniel and I moved to a different state, and he finished high school there. I went to work as an adolescent psychotherapist. I loved my job.

During our first year in our new home, Daniel went to treatment for his addiction.

My best friend, who had helped me start my new life in recovery, was graduating from college with her master's degree. My then-boyfriend and I decided to travel to another state in the upper Midwest for her graduation. After our first day on the road, I became deathly sick. I was comatose and was helicoptered to a large city hospital. I was in a coma for thirteen days, and during that time, I died and came back to life. I learned I was the second survivor of this sickness, with Jim Henson being the first. I was hospitalized in two hospitals in two different states. The second hospital was for rehabilitation. When I came out of my coma, I was 100 percent paralyzed and had to learn to use my body again. It was an experience I will never forget. My life took a turn at that time, spiritually.

My employer told my son about my illness, who then took him back to our hometown to stay. My family didn't visit me in the first hospital. My mother and Daniel came twice, once when I was first hospitalized—after the nurses and my girlfriend begged her to come because I was dying—and once when I still had a ventilator in my lungs. They only stayed about an hour after driving 325 miles. They had planned to spend the night but gave up their motel room to return home instead.

As time went by, my mother's dislike of me became part of my son's attitude toward me. He had started using drugs and alcohol again and was in an altered state most of the time. He used a lot of LSD and was a prime candidate for brainwashing. My mother relished this, and when I finally got out of the hospital, his mind was very convoluted.

Surprisingly, one day he called, asking, "Mom, can I come home and help take care of you?"

I was in awe and happily replied, "Yes!"

He returned home for a few months before moving out again to continue his chemical use. My heart was broken by his addiction and behavior. I then left the place where we had been living and returned to my hometown.

My son went to treatment again after my return. My mother, who had abused me all of my life until a few years before her death, did everything in her power to build a wall between Daniel and me. He also was a victim of her abuse—physically, verbally, emotionally. After his estrangement from me, others came forward with accountings of her abuse to him.

When Daniel was discharged from treatment, I moved to another town and began working as a psychotherapist again. My son went to a halfway house. After six months in this care, he was gainfully employed and solid in recovery. His life and mine began to feel more manageable, and I could breathe again.

In the late 1990s, I got engaged and attended college once again. I was trying to decide if I should quit my job as a therapist in a chemical dependency treatment program and finish my degree in one more year or keep on track with two more years to complete. My fiancé and I discussed my future, and I moved forward with attending school while unemployed. I had saved some money and worked a minimal amount of time with the university under a work study program. Daniel was also in college at this time and was doing well.

In 1999, my grandmother died at one hundred years of age. This was devastating for me. I wrote a short story of the memories I had of her. I was unable to read the story at the funeral, so another family member read it for me. This was my attempt to honor the woman who had truly loved me throughout my entire life and who was always there for me. During the ceremony, there was not a dry eye. One of those in attendance remarked, "I was doing pretty well until the story was read."

Grandma loved unconditionally, for she had known what it was to be a slave in her family of origin, to have little education, to be abused, and to be a servant in her married years. She loved me beyond words and continues to walk in spirit with me today. If it had not been for my grandmother's love and presence in my life, I don't dare to think what would have happened to me.

I graduated with my master's of social work degree in 2000. Shortly after this, yet another loss occurred.

One afternoon, while standing in the kitchen, talking with my fiancé, Richard, the phone rang. It was Richard's sister-in-law. She told me, in what was to be a secretive disclosure, "Richard has been coming to our house and drinking with his brother. Don't tell him that I told you that."

I replied in a very disgusted manner, "I'm not playing that game! Thank you for the information." I hung up and confronted Richard.

He said, "Yes, that is true."

"Make arrangements for another place to live," I said.

When we were dating, I told him that I had enough trauma and tragedy in my life with alcohol and drugs, and if I ever found out that he was doing either one—because he had been in recovery when we met—the relationship would be over. I had my suspicions that this had been going on for the past year, but now it was confirmed. Richard moved out three weeks later.

It seemed like an endless cycle of drama, trauma, and devastation in my life, with chemicals being the nucleus. I had fourteen years of recovery at that point, and my life was changing. Working in addiction was an eye-opener every day.

The biggest eye-opener was when Richard said, "I was in the safest position I could be. You were a counselor and didn't even know I was using."

After that, I decided to focus on healing me, my career, and helping my Daniel. I thought that if I ever became interested in someone again, I would get to know that person much better before leaping.

The day I was to present my clinical research paper (master's thesis) to the public at the university, my mother was at my house. She was going to my presentation because she would not be attending my graduation; she would be traveling with my brother to her granddaughter's graduation from a prestigious Ivy League college in the East.

I said to my mother, "You must be very proud of your children. Both of us have master's degrees."

She looked at me and said, "I am the most proud of you because you had such a hard life."

I could not believe what she'd said. I felt tears in my eyes, and they were tears of sadness because I knew what I had been through and what she had allowed.

She also said, "Alcohol and men were the most important things in my life."

I knew that to be true of her, but I was shocked when she admitted it, without any emotion attached to her words, looking straight into my eyes. She then said, "Alcohol and Daniel were the most important things in your life."

"Daniel was always the most important thing in my life," I said, "and I have been in recovery for fourteen years now. There is a big difference."

Daniel graduated from a large university shortly after I did. He and his fiancée married the next year. They then moved to a coastal state and, gradually, their lives took a drastic change. They focused on an upward trajectory in the business world while becoming acclimated to their new surroundings and friends. Daniel had worked with the rich and famous in one venue or another for many years. I had noticed the changes that were taking place, and he was now only connected to my mother; he had separated himself from family and previous friends. The air of entitlement thickened, and he finally told me, "We only want to have people in our circle who can offer us something. You have nothing to offer us."

Our relationship has been quite heartbreaking for me. Daniel became very attached to my mother and, some years later, told me that he had never bonded with me. I was shocked by this declaration. I believe my mother finally convinced him that she raised him. Daniel never wanted to hear about his childhood. I have three large Rubbermaid containers of his childhood treasures and countless photos of what he has come to deny. He expressed anger with me when I would talk about his young life.

The last time I was at his home in 2017, he was extremely rude. Before I went to the airport to return home, he became increasingly belligerent. He stood in his kitchen, screaming, hollering, and swearing at me. He kept shouting, "You are a victim!"

My only thought was, *You are a victim too, dear son*. As I looked at my grown son, I saw a young boy who felt lost in his life. I was the only safe one on whom he could spew his despair. He knew I would always love him.

He yelled about his losses—about being abused as a child and the loss of not having his brothers. My heart cried for him. When he wore his anger down, he got up from the kitchen table, walked over to me, put his arms around me, and said, "I love you, Mom. I've always been so proud of you."

I looked at him with tears in my eyes and said, "I love you, my son."

We haven't spoken since then. Daniel separated himself from his family and, along with his wife, separated from her family as well. He had always been one of my biggest cheerleaders, but he didn't realize that he was also a victim.

Unfortunately, I did not know to what degree I was subjecting Daniel to my mother's abuse of him. She was emotionally and verbally abusive to him and, at times, physically abusive. After my last visit, I sat in the airport, talking to friends and family on the phone about what had occurred during my stay. That was when I found out about my mother's abuse with him that I hadn't known about.

Our circumstances change, and the path we walk has turns and detours. I have found that where love is, nothing is ever a done deal. The light of God, the divine source of all that is, is in constant movement. The energy that surrounds each one of us, of who we are, is always in motion. If not in this lifetime, then in another. My most profound request of the universe is to let me unite with my sons again. In your glory, dear God, that Jesus will take all of our hands and lead us to the appointed place and time, that in God's unconditional love for us, we will be together. And so it is.

Several months after that last visit with Daniel and his wife, my mother died at the age of ninety-two. I was with her as she died. My brother and I took charge of her belongings and financial business. He had to go on a family business trip, however, which left me to arrange the funeral and care for her. Ironically, I sat at her bedside for three days, watching her die an agonizing death, giving her all the unconditional love that was given to me by my dear Father God.

My mother was successful in her quest to separate Daniel and me, and then she convinced him to turn away from me. In reality, what she left as her legacy is a man who has been wounded himself by tremendous emotional manipulation by the toxic behavior of an untreated alcoholic narcissist. My heart weeps for him at times and the quest for truth that he is now experiencing.

It has been over three years since my mother's death. That was my last meeting with my son. After the funeral, he waited until everyone else had gone, except for the two friends who had come with me. They both went to the car, and I walked up to my son.

He looked at me, full of despair, and hugged me. Then he said, "I love you. Take your hands off me, and don't ever touch me again. My therapist told me I shouldn't have anything to do with you." He then turned away, ran across the street while saying something that I couldn't hear, jumped into his rental car, and drove off.

My mother's last attempt at deception *after* her death was in having only my son's name on her insurance policies; she had removed my brother and I from them a few years earlier. I was very sure for many years that I would not be included in any inheritance, yet I was appointed the financial executor of her estate.

My first husband, William, who had sat with me one evening in the hospital, said several months later, "Wow, I couldn't believe how you sat there with your mom after all the shit she had done to you in your life, just telling her you loved her and holding her hand and stroking her hair."

I replied, "There was no thought involved. I just gave the love I had that she would never allow."

I have forgiven my mother for the life she endured through all of her marriages and divorces and for willingly giving her children to others to care for. It saddens my heart that she was blessed with two loving children who so longed to have a mother, but she had no skills or ability, drive, or desire to parent after she gave birth to us.

I continue to struggle with her deceptions that came between Daniel and me. Some days, I can forgive, but other days, the pain still cries inside.

4

The Medium

Behind the blindfold is a world of yesterday,

Unseen, unspoken, waiting to reveal,

Then what?

My spiritual journey led me to a medium—that is, one who has a connection with the deceased. I met this medium at a monthly gathering of healers; it was a small, rather quaint setting with several tarot card readers, a medical intuitive, past-life regression guides, shamans, energy healers, and two mediums, just to name a few. Visitors wove in and out of the practitioners, deciding who would share their fates this day. I knew many of them well, as my spiritual teacher was hosting this gathering.

I walked through the maze, searching for a friend who was a medium. I didn't see her, but another medium asked, "Can I help you?"

"I'm looking for the woman who was sitting at the table across from you," I said.

"Sadly, she was not feeling well and had to leave. Can I help you with something?"

I laughed. "Apparently, you're the person I'm to see today!" When she invited me to sit down, I told her, "I would like to connect with my mother."

When the medium opened her eyes after making the connection (which I will refer to as *coming in* and *going out*), she said, "Your mother has nothing to say to you." Then she said, "Wait a minute—someone else is coming in." She described an older woman with a shirt and pants on, holding a denim bag.

I excitedly said, "That's my grandmother, the woman who raised me."

The medium then went out and came back in, saying, "Your grandmother said, 'I attempted all of your life, until my death, to bring your mother and you back together.'"

"I knew this," I said.

Grandmother then said through the medium, "I have always loved you—always."

Now teary-eyed, I said, "Tell Grandma thank you for the love she so freely gave me and still continues to give me."

Interestingly, my mother then came in and told the medium, "I'm not sorry for anything I did in my life." My mother then told the medium that I had been an "inconvenience" to her.

My grandmother then came in and said, "I am always with you; whenever you need me, I am here."

Tears streamed down my face, and the medium said, "Can I hug you?"

"Yes," I replied.

She put her arms around me, and I could feel my grandma's hug, so warm and cuddly. When the hug was completed, the medium said, "That hug was from Grandma."

I told her, "I know." I then asked her to ask my mother two questions: "Why were you so mean to me in my life?"

And her response was, "Because I was jealous of you and wanted to hurt you."

My second question was, "Why did you want to have power and control over my son?"

She responded, "Because the only way I knew I could hurt you bad enough was by taking the one thing that you loved the most in your life."

Then Grandma quickly chimed in. "Toward the end of my life, your mother tried to keep us apart."

I told her, "I knew that, but it didn't stop me from spending every moment I possibly could with you, Grandma."

I felt all the sadness my grandmother experienced from her daughter and the unconditional love my grandma had for me. I cried many tears during that session, but they were healing, cleansing tears.

The medium then looked at me and started throwing kisses to me. She said, "These are from your grandma." That warmed my heart. The medium then said, "Grandma is surrounded by many children, and they are all laughing and playing."

Happily, I said, "My grandmother loved children, and they loved her."

Smiling, she added, "There are several cherubs fluttering around her head and shoulders, with their little tiny angel wings."

I could see this with my spiritual eye and knew she was at peace.

"Your mother is having a difficult time in her transitioning station," the medium said, "because she does not believe she did anything wrong. She will be there for some time. The lesson your mother was to learn in this life was *love*. She did not and will be back again."

"I've cut as many cords as I have been able to between her and me. I don't want to be connected with her again in any life."

She smiled. "You don't have to be. You can stay with your grandma, if you want, or in your next soul contract, you can be born into a loving family."

All I can say is, that is to be determined.

I have acknowledged my trauma and released it to source energy to complete its spiritual evolution. Sometimes, the bruises are hidden and are never allowed to heal; other times, they are brought into the light so others may heal also.

That Is Me

As darkness pulls the blanket over gray,

So do the clouds speak.

Can you feel the rain I send you to nourish the land?

Can you hear my voice as it thunders in the vibration?

Can you see my energy when my Light sparks in front of you?

Do you experience the wind as the tone of my creation?

Do not fear, but feel, listen, see, experience,

For this is only One of who I am.

When you feel the warmth of the sun upon your face,

When you hear the song of nature,

When you see the colors of the rainbow, that is me.

The sound of laughter,

The feeling of tears,

The beating of your heart,

That is also me

For whatever there is, whatever you can imagine, whatever you feel,

and whatever you see,

That is me

I AM that I AM

Each thought from me belongs to you if you claim it.

I shower with gifts, pay attention my beloved one.

What is it that you want?

The seed has been planted, in order to see it to fruition,

You must water it.

For that is me.

5

The Story of One Empath

The twisted vines of the Unseen
reveal much with an open eye

Have you ever wondered, my beautiful friend, why I spend so much time alone? Do you see me as an introvert or a recluse? Do you know that a portion of my day is feeling the energy of the earth and the tears that fall upon it? Each sound is music that fills the stillness of my life.

As I sit in the hallowed halls of my sanctuary, I feel the heartbeat of all who were here before. And in the distance, I hear my mother screaming as a nightmare that has faded. Oh, the pain she must have lived while riding the carousel of her journey, for the horses were not gaily clad but the remnants of her faded past.

I see my father running from the strength he could not find, to that bottle on the table that washed away his mind. Dear Father, how sad I was when I really saw you on your deathbed, the one man I feared the most, who melded that pathway for all the men who came within view. Only a thin, frail segment of love that you never knew.

I watched those around me as they played and had their secrets. Most of the time, I was the secret. No one knew me. Alone, I sat in a tree with the arms of the earthlings holding me as I wept for what I now know. My tears were absorbed by the air, by my body, and washed into the sea of emptiness, hoping, always hoping, that one day you would find me again and bring me home.

Time/sand memoirs—the fleeting time as sands sift through the hourglass. The irony of it is that we never know how much sand still lingers in the upper portion of the hourglass, as it stealthily continues its constant sifting.

My healing has been with time, not calculated in hours or days or even months but in recognition, in years of an unrelenting drive to feel peace. As a child of "sight," absorbing the energy around me continuously, the allowance of thoughts left a void in me when viewing others' lives. As the child peeked through the keyhole, she saw more, as if Alice, peering into the looking glass, became the journey.

In time, I realized the shift in consciousness and the ability to tune into a world beyond—the world that showed the heartbeat of the earth and the weeping of the trees, and the smile of the sun, and the mystery of the moon. I saw the colors of energy and learned that energy shape shifts as I watch energy gain denseness and form.

It is true that what you think affects all areas of life. I have witnessed events in life, and my intuition reminds me of a time when I knew this event would happen. I now chuckle to myself as I become more aware of my own being and what I am allowed to see. Sometimes, my intuition gives reference to time, but usually it is a "knowing" that an occurrence is to happen.

Ah, to see life in a glorious, sensuous stream, rejecting all that deflects from the goal. But then, what would life be without a goal? We are patterned to an expectation of milestones involving school, employment, love, marriage, children, grandchildren, retirement, and yes, even bodily death. It's the evolution of man in society and expectations. Being an empath means there are societal patterns and spiritual "awakeness." Truth, at times, has a way of showing itself before a plan is revealed.

Simply put, while we are busy making plans, life has its own ideas. My life as an empath has allowed me to see what is to come, and I have learned the magic of wearing life as a loose garment.

Color Me

Color me rainbows in the morning light,
As sun absorbs moisture from earth.
Color me sunshine as noon–day glitters,
Feeling the warmth as it lightens my soul.
Color me peace as the day now wanes,
Orchestrate music as nature sings.
Color me softness as nighttime falls,
Memories heighten, rewinding the show.

6

Spiritual Chronology, of Sorts

Through the looking glass,
A lifetime of enlightenment

This chapter is an intricate portrait of my spiritual journey—how I became who I am and why this memoir is one of healing. It is a road map that describes the unfolding of my spiritual gifts. Although my entire journey into the psychic world is not revealed in this writing, it is a sketch of what happened along the path to enlightenment. Each step brought to light a new answer and a new gift as I developed my clairvoyance, clairsentience, and claircognizance.

At the age of eleven, I was quietly working on my schoolwork in my bedroom one night. Everyone in the house was fast asleep. In the stillness, I heard a voice say my name very audibly: "Celeste, Celeste." I looked around, but no one was in sight, so I continued to focus on my schoolwork.

A few minutes later, the voice spoke again: "Celeste."

This time I answered. "Yes?"

The voice spoke clearly once more. "Work with people."

That was it; I never heard the voice again until fifty years later.

When I was nineteen, I ingested LSD and many other psychedelic drugs, drank alcohol, and smoked marijuana and cigarettes. I could see air molecules and energy waves. I felt the feelings of all whom I encountered. I saw, into the eye of the soul, what would occur in the physical in future time. What I'd seen in spirit was always the same as what later came to be in the physical realm.

I started college, and this brought a gamut of new friends who were all on the endless journey of finding themselves. This continued with heavy chemical use, love-ins (music and dancing in the park), and more questions about existence.

I now see this time not only as one of self-discovery but also one of rebellion against the establishment, the status quo of our time. In the late sixties, the quest of purpose was heavily upon my generation.

As I ventured into adulthood, I began yet another journey as I traveled to the Southwest. As I've mentioned previously, I began to study Eastern religions and, eventually, the Bible.

I would sit in the desert and the foothills with my desert friends and my dear, sacred friend, a Hopi medicine man, who was a doorway to enlightenment for me. I also had my first out-of-body experience at age twenty (in which the astral body separates from the physical body).

I was lying in my bed—my husband was at work—and I saw myself in the doorway, just hovering there, looking at me. I didn't know what was happening at the time, and I was extremely scared. Then, I was back in my body as suddenly as I'd left it. I didn't sleep for three nights after that because I didn't know what might happen to me. It was a chilling experience, one that I did not yet psychically understand.

I seemed to always know when something was going to happen, especially when a person was ready to depart this life. At that time, I did not share the metaphysical experiences I was having with anyone. Society was not ready to hear about psychics or esoteric experiences. Nor did I have the understanding to know what my experiences were at the time.

For several years, I continued to experience these metaphysical phenomena. I have seen myself gazing through a thin veil, the veil that separates dimensions, and have seen humans currently existing in a third-dimensional frame of reference. I have been elevated to a much higher dimension through sight, through a third-eye view of the future in this dimension. As of this writing, I have seen an extraordinary series of events unfold, and as earth's time frame continues, more is revealed each day.

One incident involved seeing my ex-husband, who is now deceased, as the father of a baby boy. He had remarried after our divorce. I saw him about a year after my near-death experience, and I asked, "Do you and your wife have a baby boy?"

He shook his head. "No, we don't have any children."

A few months after his death, his wife gave birth to a baby boy. This is only one example of my prophetic gifts.

When I was in a comatose state, I saw another incredible scene—many people in a huge parking lot–type setting, with a row of shops on two sides of a rather dismal-looking area. The people walked quickly, not paying attention to anyone else or talking to anyone. All were dressed in blue, and I knew many of those I saw. A wall of water rose up next to this mall area, with white foam on its tip, surging straight up into the air. Its height had no measurement in the spirit world, so my human calculation is unavailable.

The lights on the power poles emitted sparks, and as I looked up, I saw Jesus hovering in the pale-blue sky, viewing all that was happening on earth. The colors I saw around him were pastel colors—blues, pinks, yellows, lavenders. I believe what I saw was how those on earth were interacting with each other, the collective humankind—no interactions, singular, without care for one another.

The stores represented the disposable society we have created, without knowledge of what this planet and its life are about. Interacting with others is chiefly through technology, and humans have lost the kindred spirit, the spirit of who we are. Texting and emailing or social media has been substituted for human contact.

The water represents the *elemental undines*, or mermaids, who have taken control of the seas, as a reaction to humankind's wastefulness and pollution of the waters. The elements—fire, water, air, and earth—react to the wasteful behaviors of humankind. In my near-death journey, the water was the wall that was telling humankind, "No more," but they did not listen. As the water mixes with the other elements, the rage of what we have created on this planet relentlessly warns of disaster.

Humankind is not listening and, sadly, may be crushed from the weight of its own denial.

The above examples are just two of the scenes I was shown. It is common for me now to see premonitions of what is and what will be. My senses have developed quite keenly to receive messages from source energy.

In the late '90s, as I previously revealed, I foretold the death of my grandmother, who was three months into her one hundredth year on this planet, to my son and mother.

My out-of-body experiences happened more often after that. I did not know when they were going to happen. Sometimes, I would start leaving my body when I was driving; sometimes at work; sometimes at home. It didn't seem to matter what was happening.

Early one morning, as I was driving to work, I started feeling somewhat disoriented and could not drive any farther. I had an idea of what was happening. A dear friend of mine, who lived on the East Coast, was very concerned about a surgery his father was having that morning. I knew I was picking up on his energy. I pulled the car over on the shoulder and called my friend. He was at the hospital, awaiting the upcoming surgery.

I told him, "You need to take some deep, relaxing breaths, pray for your father, and know that God is in charge." I was then able to resume my drive to work.

After arriving at work, I was readying myself for a business meeting when, suddenly, his energy swept over me like a tornado. I was unable to focus, and I thought, *I have to get to the business meeting. I need help!* I closed my eyes and asked, "Grandmother, come into my view in the spirit world. I need help!" I saw my friend's energy coming toward me in spirit, and my grandmother stood in front of me with her arms outstretched in front of her. Lightning bolts came from the palms of her hands that acted as a block against the energy. As I watched this spectacular scene, I thanked her, and the energy between my friend and me was cut off.

I then swiftly went to my meeting. When I arrived, my supervisor looked quite concerned and asked, "Are you OK?"

Somewhat breathless, I said, "I will be."

She winked. "All right." She knew of my gifts and didn't question me any further.

Later that morning, I called my friend, and he said that his father had come through the surgery just fine.

"Told you he would be OK," I said.

One evening, after attending a presentation, a friend, who sat across from me, said, "I was watching you during the presentation. Your eyes were open, but they were glossy-looking. Are you OK?"

I told her about my out-of-body experiences and then said, "My soul was not there at the time."

She looked astonished. "Are you all right?"

I laughed. "I am. I've been doing this for at least twenty years now, and I always come back."

My friend didn't say anything then. Later, she became quite cognizant of these potential happenings, and when she noticed, she would say, "Celeste, Celeste, are you OK?"

I would look at her, dazed, and say, "Yes, I'm fine."

Finally, I confided in a mentor who is a Healing Touch practitioner (healing using chakras and energy). "I've been having out-of-body astral experiences since I was twenty years old," I told her. "I also know and sense things that are going to happen. I can look at people and 'see' their lives."

She was somewhat taken back but said, "Learning to 'ground' yourself may help. Carry a hematite crystal with you all the time."

"Where do I find hematite?"

"It will come to you," she said.

Not long after that, I was at a spiritual fair and saw a counter covered by many crystals; I found hematite.

My mentor aided me with grounding, and I was able to control the out-of-body experiences much better.

I found it very important to keep myself grounded at all times. I envision tree roots coming out from the bottoms of my feet, going deep down into the ground, into the very core of Mother Earth, and connecting to a large blue-crystal boulder. This practice keeps me connected to the earth realm.

I explored my experiences and started going to spiritual fairs and having tarot and oracle card readings. I visited with shamans and had healing on my body from the spirit world. I was now on a more heightened spiritual quest to find out about me. All of my life, I knew I was different but did not understand it. Every speaker I heard resonated with me. I was hungry for knowledge.

One of my most memorable encounters was with a Hmong shaman at a spirituality conference I attended. This beautiful young woman asked, "Would you please stand in front of me and close your eyes?" After a few minutes, she softly said, "You have three patches over your eyes. I removed two patches from one of your eyes, but you will have to remove the third patch yourself." She then smiled and said encouragingly, "Archangel

Michael always walks beside you on your right side, and your grandmother walks beside you on your left side."

Words of gratitude spoke from my heart. "Thank you so much."

My friend who attended the conference with me was in awe of this healing. Excitedly, she could not wait to ask, "Can you tell a difference?"

I smiled and winked. "Not at this time, but spiritually, I will come to know if it is true."

I did feel peace at this time and knew something definitely had changed within me.

Later that day, I attended a large group session with a medium. This was my first experience with mediumship, and I was quite excited. The medium had two segments to the session: the first was an opportunity to ask a question about a person, living or deceased. We were instructed to raise our hands if we wanted to be chosen. I was rather hesitant, but after a few people had asked questions, I raised my hand.

"I would like to know about my grandmother."

She closed her eyes and crossed over into the spirit realm through her third eye. When she opened her eyes, she hesitated a moment but then said, "I usually don't do this during a group session, but your grandmother has not crossed over yet. I will help her do that." She turned around with her back to the group, and I saw her body shaking. When she turned to face the group again, she smiled at me. "You should be very happy. You helped your grandmother to cross over today."

I started to cry, and the medium also had tears. With moist eyes and a grateful heart, I whispered, "Thank you so much for helping my grandma." I marveled at what she "saw," and as she saw others, I also experienced that with her. Today, she is my friend.

A year later, two of my friends were doing Healing Touch on me, and they unknowingly checked my nodal line—the karmic direction of the body's lifeline.

"Your nodal line is dark and cloudy. I recommend finding a healer that clears Akashic records." Akashic records are a compendium of all actions, thoughts, and words ever to have occurred in the past, present, or future. They are recorded in a spiritual plane, or etheric plane—the energetic waves or frequencies vibrated in the void.

About two months after my friend suggested I should have my Akashic records cleared, I attended a Women's Spirituality Conference and was led to a psychic who could orchestrate that clearing.

She asked me, "What led you to me?"

Quietly, I told my story. "Two women who did Healing Touch on me recommended that I have my Akashic records cleared. They saw that my nodal line was dark."

"I can check your records," the psychic said. "If I see something that I think won't be advantageous for you to know or that's dangerous, I won't give you that information."

I agreed. As I sat across from her, she closed her eyes, and her body began to shake. I felt a surge from my feet to my head, and tears streamed down my face.

When she opened her eyes, she asked, "How are you?"

All I could do was stammer, "I'm—I'm okay. I feel very light and free."

"I cleared everything, and it is nice and bright now. I will only tell you that you have lived many past lives, and you were a teacher in some of those lives. Sometimes, it was not safe for you." She then adamantly said, "The patch that you still have over your eye is thinning, and I can see your eyeball through it. When it is gone, you will come into your full psychic gifts."

I was shocked that she saw the patch over my eye that the Hmong shaman had mentioned a year earlier. It was a cleansing experience that allowed me to feel the release of timeless clutter—some quite toxic—that had been blocking my path to healing.

When my friend who had accompanied me to the conference saw me, she exclaimed, "Oh, my God! What happened to you?" I told her what I'd experienced with my clearing, and she said, "You look like a different person!"

After that, I spent as much time attending spiritual fairs and conferences as I could. I was like a sponge for spirituality. I wanted to know about myself and who I was beyond the body. Every time I sat with a tarot card reader or healer, they would always finish with, "You know you are psychic." I had yet to learn exactly what I was capable of doing or any terms for what was happening with me.

Three years ago, I met a man at a nightclub in a Twin Cities suburb who changed my life. I watched him walk in with an entourage of people hovering around him. He and his troupe sat two tables away from me. It was my birthday, and I was there with several friends that evening. I was feeling happy and joyful. I love to dance, and I did—to every song that was played until we left that evening.

At one point, whispers raced through the crowd, and soon, this man was asked to come on stage and sing a song with the band that was performing that evening. He was sharply dressed, wearing black slacks, a white shirt, and a black vest. He also wore a black bandana on his head and had an earring in each ear. His brown skin glistened on stage.

I was very impressed by his presence and voice, but more importantly, he kept looking at me—and I at him. When the song finished, he humbly jumped off the stage. After the break, he again was asked to join the band in a song and went back on stage.

At this time, the club was full of people, and when he went on stage again, everyone ran onto the dance floor. This time, however, no one danced; instead, they all got out their phones and took pictures of him. I was oblivious to his fame, but I took my camera and went onto the dance floor with everyone else. I thought, *I should take a picture because that's what others are doing.*

The mystery singer shone like a radiant star—I still didn't know who he was—as he sang Prince's song "Purple Rain." He was phenomenal. When he finished, everyone cheered, and he walked back to his table and sat down. Many who had been sitting with him were next to the stage as he sang. I noticed a name on the back of a jacket that one his entourage was wearing, but it meant nothing to me at the time.

When the song was finished, the band took a break. They had been taking long breaks, twenty to thirty minutes in duration. As I walked back to my table, I noticed a person was sitting in the aisle, almost as a barrier next to the singer, to prevent anyone from getting near him.

I didn't think much about it, but suddenly, not of my own volition, I walked right over to his table. The person in the aisle seemed to have vanished before my eyes, and I leaned down next to the singer's ear and whispered, "Thank you for making my birthday so special tonight."

He looked up at me. "What is your name?"

"Celeste."

He then stood up, looked me in the eyes, put his arms around me, and held me.

Everything that happened that night was not done by me but by spirit. He and I elevated into, I am guessing, the twelfth dimension, which is "Christ consciousness," where only the energy of love exists. When we stopped holding each other, he took my hand and then pulled me into him again and held me, heart to heart; we began deep breathing in unison.

Nothing existed; there were no other people, no sounds to where we had elevated. This happened three times, with us holding each other, and then him taking my hand, pulling me in again, and holding my hand. After our third embrace, he held my hand and looked at me with an intense sadness; it was a look of, "I just found you, and now you are leaving me."

I removed his hand from mine ever so gently. We bowed to each other, honoring each other, and then I turned and walked away. I was completely aware of my surroundings but was not grounded in any way.

When I arrived at my table, I said to my friend, "Did you see what just happened there?"

She had been outside, getting some fresh air, and had no idea what I was talking about. Remember that the band took twenty- to thirty-minute breaks, so during that entire break, my dear Spirit Light (as I came to refer to him) and I embraced in another dimension.

When the band started performing again, I went out to dance. I saw him getting up to leave, and I thought I should do something. After all, I had just had one of the most incredible experiences of my life with him. I went back to my table to get my phone. Still being very elevated spiritually, I looked at him, and he was looking at me. I held up my phone. He held up his index finger, indicating he needed a minute; then he walked over to me.

I asked if I could take a picture of us, but I absolutely could not function to do so. Our energies together were too heavy for me to operate the camera on my phone.

My friend then walked up and said, "Give me that phone. I'll take your pictures."

As we stood with our arms around each other, she took our picture. He turned, softly whispered good night, and left the building.

That was it. I had no idea with whom I'd had this most incredible experience.

When my girlfriend and I left the nightclub, I asked her to google the name I'd seen on the back of the jacket. To my surprise, this man was quite famous, and I was still hovering in spirit as we floated back home. Due to confidentiality, I am unable to reveal the birth name of this amazing man and always refer to him only as Spirit Light, as that is who he has always been to me.

At one point, my friend asked if I was OK with driving.

Surprised, I looked over at her. "Am I doing something wrong?"

My friend laughed. "No, I was just wondering. You are very high."

We found our way home by angel power that night!

Upon my arrival at home, I looked my spiritual mystery man up in Messenger on my phone, and there he was! I sent him the picture of us and again told him, "Thank you for making my birthday so special."

The next morning, I awoke to find a friend request from him on Facebook and also a message from him in Messenger. He wrote, "The honor was mine. I knew when I entered the building last night there was a very strong empath there."

We became instant friends. He asked, "Would you give me permission to view the Akashic records about possible past lives together?"

I was also interested and said, "Of course."

He messaged me later and happily reported, "We have had many lives together. I was your husband in one life, your father in another, and your canine in another."

We have spent hours talking about our current lives and past lives. It is amazing to have this beautiful bond with each other in this lifetime and to have found each other again.

We love each other deeply; he is my Spirit Light. He has taught me much about myself. A psychic told me that he had come back for me this time.

During one of our conversations, I thanked him for coming back for me.

"Even though the first few chapters were quite challenging," he said, "I would not have missed it for the world."

I have a profound connection with him, and he has guided me farther into the light.

I later shared this phenomenal experience with my dear friend and then–mentor, who was the Healing Touch practitioner. She had always guided me in my spiritual journey. She was a few years older than I was and carried much wisdom from her life and experiences from the healing work she does. She is also the mentor who guided me to begin training with Healing Touch.

As I talked about Spirit Light, she became more curious. She saw the change in me and the hunger I had to learn about who I was. One evening, after I had finished messaging with my dear Spirit Light, my phone rang, and it was my friend. Our conversation became quite serious, and she then told me, "You need to get connected with a psychic who can teach you about who you are. No one around here has the gifts that you have, and we cannot help you any more."

I felt abandoned and alone, except for my beautiful new soul mate. A few short months later, an amazing psychic teacher appeared to me. I contacted her and told her what I was looking for. I began an extremely intense spiritual journey with her.

Since then, I have moved from the town where I was living to be near her and my beautiful Spirit Light. I have never called him by his name unless I am introducing him to someone.

I also have a love—I've been with him for the past five and a half years—who brought me to the city of my past once more. He is the light that shines in my heart. Over two years ago, he experienced a hemorrhagic stroke, and his recovery has been one of relearning. He has been residing in a care center since it occurred. Our spiritual connection is incredibly strong, and we are able to elevate ourselves from this space-time continuum into a free-floating dimension, where frequency is fluid, and our spirits can dance with and around each other in lucid motion.

We cherish that feeling and bathe in it, as if in water that has the gentle movement of a soft wave, bringing us in motion with each other. This is what brings joy to us when we cannot be together. I know that he is always with me, riding the same delicious wave.

I could not imagine being without him, for we also have been together in countless lifetimes, not because of karmic ties but because we just love each other, although there is always something to learn in spirit and on earth school. At times, I feel him so intensely that I cannot function, and I have to tell him to stop thinking about me so intently because I can't do whatever I'm doing. He is magic to me, and I to him.

A Dimensional Journey

> As I breathe in new breath,
> So too do I breathe in a new Light

As my pathway continues to weave its intricate pattern, I am led to a variety of healers who compassionately help me to heal my soul. It is metaphysical and etheric work. You may be unfamiliar with what I am about to disclose, but again, I speak of the spirit world and being psychic; this language is who I am.

Approximately three years ago, I became connected to my heart and saw the fear it housed within. A solid armor of darkness surrounded it, extending from current times to past lifetimes. I had difficulty with my heart and knew something was causing the problem, but I wasn't yet aware of it.

One afternoon, I was listening to meditation music; I started feeling weak and had to sit down. As I sat and closed my eyes, tears started forming. I then saw my heart and watched as it slowly began to open its heart eye, allowing the doorway of its center to invite the light to come in. I cried as I saw the blocks to love that had been present for so long, and I knew why. I sat in reverence as I honored my heart space, watching the beautiful magenta light of my inner heart meld with the radiant emerald-green light of my outer heart, emitting a brilliant light that penetrated the blocks as they crumbled. My tears of joy washed away the heaviness, the burden of the past, and I sat in ecstasy, breathing into my loving heart space that was now open. I felt complete lightness.

The recognition of my life as the mirror of my soul has allowed me to do some deep diving into the old blockages. This inner work has opened the doors to the boundless, endless mirroring to occur.

Since then, I have had several past-life regressions. I will address a few that involve my current love. Past lives reveal our souls' incarnations and the type of beings we have been. At times, we are human; other times, our souls are other beings.

My journey with my current love has been one of incredibly ancient times, now finding its way into the present. I am unable to share in binary language some of these lifetimes because I am not privilege to that information.

I was told that I was once a being (one of material substance) in space that was self-sustaining, somewhat like a planet only a being. My current love's (Trey's) soul was with me, although his being was not self-sustaining and relied upon me for his substance.

In another lifetime, we were two white pyramids; one was my energy, and the other was his energy. From the top of our pyramids, a dark-blue light rose up to the heavens. Our blue light connected with a purple light that formed a bridge between us, with purple rain. The individual guiding this past life transmission said she heard the song "Purple Rain" at the time. I have been told many times that the energy between us is very strong, and we love each other very much.

As our journey continued, past life brought us to earth. Because we are sometimes males and sometimes females or even animals, including different colors and nationalities in other lives, in one life, I was a black man, and Trey was a white woman. We were adolescents, walking down an earthen pathway. Trey wore a beautiful white dress and white bonnet with ruffles and lace. I had something very important to talk to her about, and when she turned to face me, I saw it was my current love. I felt the tears as I realized who it was, and the figure disappeared.

Another life we shared was quite treacherous and heartbreaking. I was told about this past life after I was diagnosed with bladder cancer, had surgery, but continued to feel a heaviness in my abdomen. It was as if there was a congestion or something pressuring my pelvic region.

During this past life, Trey and I were both black, and I was pregnant. A group of white men had savagely raped me and used tools to tear apart my body and rip out my baby. Trey was there, being restrained as he witnessed this. The white men killed my baby, and then they killed Trey. It was devastating to me, but in my past-life regression, divine-source energy had been asked that I not feel but only be aware of what had happened to me. When I came out of the spirit world after seeing this, my abdomen and pelvic region no longer felt the heaviness, the congestion, that had been prominent before this regression. The sadness I experienced stayed with me quite heavily for some weeks as I thought about our connection and what we had experienced. My bond to him grew stronger from knowing this, although he had no knowledge of it, and I have yet to tell him.

Another of my lives was as an early pioneer girl. My parents and I lived in a plains setting, with only tall grasses and brush around. We had a simple wooden, unpainted house. My father was a very kind and compassionate man but said very little. My mother was happy and joyful. She loved life and would dance with me in our small living space quite often, as my father sat at the bare wooden table in the kitchen and smiled. The next scene I saw was a very dark corner of a room, and my mother lay in a bed with white sheets and a brown blanket. Her head was propped up with three pillows, and she wore a white dressing gown and a white sleeping bonnet. I saw myself sitting next to her bed on an old wooden chair, with my hands in my lap, looking at her. I stood up, walked to the head of the bed, and looked into her face. It was the face of my grandmother who had raised me in my current life. The last thing I remember is saying, "You were my mother all along!" I came out of that regression very happy to know that my dear grandmother had been my mother in the past.

These are only a few examples of what I have seen and what has helped me to heal in this lifetime. Our souls, our spirits, always remember. At times, we have feelings of déjà vu or precognition, but in my career of psychotherapy, it is not recognized, even though many will say, "That was déjà vu."

The workshop I developed about women, empowerment, and spirituality delves into the hidden subconscious and allows the consciousness of what has been buried to be recognized, which is the avenue of healing that transpires. Here is where freedom, confidence, and clarity allow and release the truth of you.

Through my work with my spirit mentor and my guides, I was given direction to reunite with my eternal soul child who has been with me throughout eternity. Initially, my guides told me to meditate on this connection. Once I was able to visualize her, I began talking to her from my heart in a most loving and compassionate space. In the beginning, I had to coax her from the cave she lived in. I saw her peeking at me from the entrance of the cave, shy and somewhat untrusting. At that point, I spoke to her: "I am so sorry that you had to carry the burden and heartache for all of my lifetimes." I told her this over and over. Slowly, she began trusting me and inched her way from the only protection she had ever known, the cave she lived in.

My spirit mentor encouraged me to talk to my eternal child more than once a day and tell her often, "I love you so much. Thank you. I'm sorry for you having to carry the burden for all of eternity." As the days and weeks passed, my little one became more familiar and trusting of me. Then, one day, she walked up to me, put her hand on my leg when I was sitting down, and looked up at me with her soft, beautiful eyes. She had long blonde hair, and she allowed me to stroke her hair as I talked to her, always thanking her and saying, "You no longer have to carry the burdens of the past. I will take care of us now."

She carried so much heartache. I understand why it took us time to reconnect. I talk to her often now, especially when I am sad, because she is right next to me, ready to carry that burden again. I let her know, "It's all right. Even if I am hurting, I will carry the burden of that pain." I now take care of her; I tell her she is beautiful, and her little light shines.

It's not easy work to delve into with oneself. You must travel within, be willing to write down the pain, look at it, and realize that it has never been about you or who you are in this lifetime; it's about them, all of them, not you. Feel the sadness, the grief, the loss—at least in this lifetime—of not having love, care, or compassion from those who were to be the foundation of life.

In my marriages, which both occurred during my years of addiction, I wondered why. Why did all of this happen? I walked on, knowing that if there is something inside that doesn't feel good, change it! This reunion with my eternal soul child has brought about great peace and freedom.

Whenever I start feeling lost, I remind myself that as much as I am in charge through free will, I am also quite dependent upon source energy in living my life. Spirit is most eager to help me, whether it be the divine source, God, Lord Jesus, my beautiful holy angels, my guides, my intuition, or my elementals.

Jesus said he would give his angels charge over me, and I trust that (Psalm 91:11). They are always available and never leave me. We are never alone ever. Our guardian angels are always with us, and our spirit guides act as a guide to us during our entire lives here on this planet.

I have spent considerable time doing present and generational healing of my soul. It needs it, and the time has come. I have been able to release so much that has kept me trapped for so long. I see much in meditation. I also work with spiritual teachers who suggest avenues to explore. There are volumes of writing about feelings, thoughts, behaviors, goals, wants, desires, traps, and forward movement. It is strenuous work, but my walking out from the cave and into the light has been exhilarating, with newfound joy surrounded by love on all sides.

I am willing now to let it all go. At one time, I had fear of doing so because I did not know what it meant to truly release the past or perhaps even the stuck feelings I had. It is easy for ego to slip back in and attempt to judge and manipulate a situation because of old thought patterns and training we have been led to believe. This is a time in my life of unlearning. We all need unlearning and connection with our true spiritual beings. There is so much love swirling around us at all times, waiting to connect with another.

The age of Aquarius, with which I resonated during the late 1960s and early 1970s, is now coming to fruition. The darkest of times are upon us, which is a contrast to the light that is making itself known in the world at this time. In writing this memoir in 2020, according to numerology, it was a 4 year—a year of home, a solid foundation, security, and safety. Making these things work is the mainstream of survival. At this time, we continue to experience a pandemic; racial unrest with inequality at its helm, led by the outdated heresy of white supremacy; and governmental wars with insurgence, stemming from the pits of the old, worn-out, irrelevant, nonsensical rhetoric that has run its course. The discord that has been on this planet for millennia is now transitioning into the fifth dimension.

In 2021, we are in a universal five year, an energy of instability, and a mandate of change. It is a time of self-realization. The door is opening, and the light is shining through. Move forward now with fortitude, like the warrior. We are the change that is needed in this world.

Take My Hand

Take my hand, my sheepish friend, and I will lead you to a place,
Once called Neverland,
A place we all can play and feel the joy of who we are,
A circle of likeness and togetherness,
Building on a Ray of Light,
Making up each soul, for we are all in fact,
One.

7

The Dark Ball of Energy

It is in Releasing and Allowing that
Freedom is Found

In 2004, I noticed a dark ball of energy floating around inside my body. I was fifty-four years old, and I had been under tremendous stress for the majority of my life. Sickness was a state of mind and body with which I was quite familiar.

The following is what I experienced in a ten-year span of health challenges, which I coined as the *dark ball of energy* that traveled through my body. This ball of energy was a darkness or illness that I intuitively felt within my body.

The dark ball of negative energy that traveled around inside my physical body had been absorbed by my etheric body (my spirit) and found its way inward, until it became a collective ball of dark energy, its main goal being to attack the host—me—causing a ruination of my physical and emotional being.

I had spent decades meditating and looking within, becoming conscious of my inner self. As I became aware of this energy, I meditated on what I was feeling within. I saw the energy and dark color in each area where it stopped as an illness or disease.

The stress in my life was once again affecting me in ways I didn't yet understand. At the beginning of this time span, the dark ball of energy was mainly focused in my heart region.

During 2004, I began feeling very exhausted. I had started working on a project with which I had little experience, but I liked the challenge. I had been asked by the hospital board to develop an adult-outpatient chemical-dependency treatment program for the hospital. I spent ten or more hours per day, sometimes seven days a week, for several months, writing the program—policies and procedures, educating hospital staff, media coverage, program space, and creating a brochure, just to name a few of the necessities of opening a new program. I was exhausted.

I started noticing shortness of breath, then light-headedness and dizziness. I was admitted to the emergency room, and in the days that followed, a protocol was outlined to test my heart at Mayo Clinic in Rochester, Minnesota. I was diagnosed with atrial fibrillation. Immediately, I was prescribed the blood thinner warfarin and had weekly blood tests to monitor its effectiveness. My diet had stabilized, and I had prescribed medication for my blood pressure, but I still experienced tiredness, dizziness, and shortness of breath.

My cardiologist then suggested that I consider a cardioversion to shock my heart back into normal sinus rhythm (regular heartbeat). This procedure was done by inserting a tube with a camera down my throat, into an area where my heart could be monitored when my heart was stopped. My heart was then started again by adhering pads to my chest and back and administering paddles to jump-start it. After this procedure, my heart was in a normal sinus rhythm. I continued with the prescribed heart medication and blood-thinning medication to prevent blood clots.

I felt much better as a result of having the cardioversion performed, and my energy returned. Life, again, was great! I continued with the implementation of the chemical-dependency program. As a result of my working in the community for several years with Court Services and Human Services, my program was at full capacity. I was employed by this hospital for three years. At that time, the hospital was in the planning stages of building a new hospital, and the treatment program was not part of the new vision; it subsequently was dismantled.

It was during this time that I was led on another journey, one of self-discovery. It was not planned, but I had procrastinated much too long with looking openly at family difficulties and how I had been affected by family behaviors, as well as my own behaviors. I would recommend that those in recovery from mood-altering chemicals not procrastinate on this.

At the age of fifty-four, after eighteen years of being free of alcohol and drug use, I decided it was time to complete the fourth step from *The Big Book* of Alcoholics Anonymous.

Step 4: Made a searching and fearless moral inventory of ourselves.

I met a speaker at an AA conference at that time who became a close friend; in reality, I believe he is part of my soul family. He encouraged me to do this step and guided me through the process by phone calls from his home on the East Coast, emails, and text messages. It took me a year to complete this heart-wrenching process.

As I started to write my moral inventory, I began to have nightmares and had to stop for a few months. One day, I received a phone call from Alec, my fourth-step guide, and he thought it was time for me to continue writing again, so I did.

It was painful to relive my past. I shed many tears and had nightmare-type dreams about what had been my life. As I neared the end of the fourth step, Alec connected me with Kim, a woman who lived in a city near me, to complete the last section, which addressed sexuality. He knew Kim would be able to guide me soundly through its finality. When I finished, I had ninety-four pages of my life on paper. I was drained physically from writing, drained mentally from remembering my entire life and writing it down on paper, drained emotionally from the feelings generated in remembering, and drained spiritually from facing my life once again. I always was connected to God and Alec while I did this work.

One of the questions I answered in the inventory was, "What was the anger like in your home as a child?" I wrote at length about the physical, emotional, and verbal abuse I received; about the abandonment and rejection; of being moved from my home at six months of age and living in a variety of situations in different towns and states. Finally, I wrote about the brutal beatings I witnessed by my father and stepfather toward my mother.

I met Kim in a park between her city and mine. She was very kind and compassionate. We sat across from each other at an old wooden picnic table, and I read my ninety-four-page moral inventory to her, which was, in fact, known as the fifth step. We spent three hours that afternoon, talking about my fourth step. See fifth step, below:

> Step 5: Admit to God, to ourselves, and to another human being the exact nature of our wrongs.

After we finished, I drove home, meditated for an hour, reviewed what I had presented for my fifth step, and proceeded to completion by doing steps six and seven. I sat for an hour in complete quietness, meditating on whether I had anything else to add to my fourth and fifth steps. I did not. At that point, I completed step 6. I then asked God to remove my shortcomings, the defects of character, that I might go on to live a life of freedom from my past. That was the completion of step 7.

Step 6: Were entirely ready to have God remove all these defects of character.

Step 7: Humbly asked Him to remove our shortcomings.

At that time, I felt as if an extreme burden had been lifted from me. The loving and nurturing attitude Kim had with me that day in the park was a significant turning point in my healing.

I spoke with a friend, who was another recovering alcoholic, as well as a Catholic priest. I asked him, as a man with knowledge of the Bible, "If I am truly sorry for my past behaviors and never do them again, am I forgiven?"

He told me I was forgiven. I could truly feel those words resonating in my heart.

In early 2020, I received a communication from Alec, who had been instrumental in helping me with my fourth step: "My belief is that there is much more revelation outside of the twelve-step framework. Deep-seated trauma, repair of our psyche, is not within that framework. Do not let ego lead the way."

I marveled at the insight he had obtained in the past several years and thanked him for his humble disclosure.

After spending an exhaustive amount of time reliving my past during my fourth- through seventh-step work of exploration, I saw how the trauma had a significant bearing on my health. I focused on this dark ball of energy and noticed a consistent pattern. In each area of my body where this ball of energy stopped, I developed an illness or disease that needed immediate attention.

I continued life with multiple health problems. After the treatment center, where I was employed, closed, I accepted a position with a major medical center as a behavioral-health case manager. There were two of us in this position, and I carried dual licenses as a licensed independent clinical social worker and a licensed alcohol and drug counselor. Because of these credentials, my focus was primarily patients with chemical-dependency issues. My coworker's focus was patients with mental-health diagnoses. Each of us had patients with both diagnoses; many of the patients referred to us were dually diagnosed with mental and chemical health issues.

I continued to be quite ill during my years of employment with this medical center, until my last year in this capacity. I was under tremendous stress yet again in my work area, for a variety of reasons.

Unfortunately, that dark ball of energy kept moving. This time it stopped around the area of my navel. I had an incision that went all the way down the front of my body from a surgery in 1980, when my spleen was removed due to having a blood disease called hereditary spherocytosis. My red blood cells are sphere-shaped instead of round, and the spleen was eating my red blood cells, viewing them as being foreign objects in my body because of their shape. Another incision on top of that was made when I had my appendix removed while in a coma from my near-death experience in 1994, along with having a heart catheter in place. This was the area where the next medical problem occurred.

Each area where a stitch had gone into the skin on my abdomen became herniated. I had a horrific cough when I traveled to Hawaii, which caused trauma to that area, and the consistent muscle expansion from coughing opened the incision area of my abdomen from the inside. My intestine started coming through the underlying areas of tissue.

During this same time, I also experienced pain on my right side below my ribs. This dark ball of energy had been bouncing back and forth. The physician working with me at Mayo Clinic was aware of the multiple hernias, and he now diagnosed me with having gallbladder attacks. After a conversation about this situation, my doctor said, "Removing the gallbladder is of first importance." Surgery was scheduled for a few days later, due to my being on blood thinners, which had to be out of my system before surgery could happen.

I awoke two days later to the sound of my alarm. I opened my eyes and stretched, but when I tried to sit up in bed, I experienced extreme pain in my abdomen. My intestine was bulging out from my abdomen, just below and to the right of my belly button. I could not bend my body. I attempted to push the intestine back in, as I had been able to do in the past, but it would not budge. I rolled onto my side and somehow slid out of bed and to my feet. I finally was able to stand, but I felt panicky. *What to do?* It is baffling how the mind is able to control the body, and I was able to get dressed, get into my car, and drive to work, forty miles from my home.

When I arrived at work, I described to one of the nurses what was happening and was taken to the emergency room at Mayo Clinic immediately. As things sometimes happen, due to the extreme emergency of the possibility of my intestine twisting and getting blocked, it ended up being the first surgery. I had to wait three days before having surgery to ensure the blood thinner was no longer in my system and that my blood had thickened enough to clot normally. During the three-day hospitalized wait, I was only able to lie flat on my back so the intestine would be at rest.

A twenty-centimeter mesh screen was implanted in my abdomen for hernia repairs, and it has served my body well. At times, I feel the intestine but nothing that causes concern.

After this surgery, my doctor said, "I want to wait eight weeks before performing the gallbladder surgery so your body has some time to heal."

Six weeks later, the gallbladder became an emergency episode for surgery. I was experiencing excruciating pain on the right side under my rib cage, and the doctor said she would remove my gallbladder now. The plan to wait eight weeks turned into an immediate lifesaving procedure I had to take. Extreme measures were taken due to the blood thinners still in my body.

My poor body was so rundown, and I was exhausted from the onslaught of medical problems. It seemed as if my body had been doing a significant purging of the old toxic feelings I had been experiencing, and I started feeling freedom from the past. Having an awareness of how the mind/body is affected by past trauma, I gained insight of how I carried the past within.

On Thanksgiving Day, a year later, my brother and his wife hosted a celebratory feast at their home. I was looking forward to the turkey stuffed with dressing and the pecan pie that my sister-in-law would make. She was a wonderful baker, and I was excited. They were expecting approximately twenty-five family members, and I was looking forward to visiting with them all.

While driving down the highway to his home, I blacked out. It was only momentary, and when my awareness returned, I was still driving in the correct lane—but I was scared. I didn't know what had happened, and cognitively, I couldn't reason enough to know that I should pull over and call my brother or anyone else. I just kept driving and saying to myself, "You are OK. Just keep driving. You are OK. Just keep driving," over and over to get to my destination.

I want to emphasize that I was *scared*! My mind was numb, and I was not fully cognizant of what had happened or why. When I arrived at his house I attempted to walk to the front door and had to stop three times to get enough breath to continue on. When I reached the door, I could only ring the doorbell. My sister-in-law opened the door, looked at me, and yelled for my brother. He came running and immediately put me in his car and drove me to the hospital Emergency Department.

En route, I was able to say, "Everything will happen very quickly, so just stand aside." I wanted him to know what to expect so he wasn't frightened by the fast pace of what was to happen. I was admitted to the hospital in order to explore the reason for the blackout.

Once again, tests were performed to see how my heart was functioning—electrocardiogram and echocardiogram, resulting in my heart reverting to atrial fibrillation. My heart, due to being in a–fib, was experiencing abnormally long spaces between beats. My doctor said, "I would like to do another cardioversion to see if I can get your heart to stay in normal sinus rhythm."

After this cardioversion, my consciousness seemed a bit disoriented. I was assured that I would feel better in a few days. After discharge from the hospital, I was back to work again a week later. My body and mind were functioning in sync, and I did very well for six months.

My heart again reverted, and a third cardioversion was performed. This time, my chest and back were slightly burned from the pads used to restart my heart, and the cognitive orientation took longer to resolve. I told my cardiologist that I would not have another cardioversion unless it was a life-or-death situation. This time, my heart did not regain normal sinus rhythm. I remained on heart medication and blood thinners.

My intuition was always aware when the dark ball of energy was activating again in my body. Because of the energy work I had been doing for a few years with chakras, or energy portals, located within the body, I could not only feel this energy but also see it in meditation. Each area where the dark ball stopped was a dark-colored area in my body.

The next area where this ball settled was in another area of my abdomen, and I became very ill. A constant feeling of nausea was present daily, and I could not eat. My hair started to fall out, and I was extremely weak. I had no idea what was causing this to happen, but I saw the darkness in my body.

I visited my doctor at least weekly, and she performed minimal blood tests. She kept telling me at each visit that there were no unusual findings, yet I was becoming sicker as the days progressed.

Then one day, I received a telephone call from my doctor's nurse, who said, "The doctor asked me to call you to tell you that she hasn't found any problem areas in the tests she has done."

I couldn't believe what I was hearing. I said, "There *is* something wrong with me. I continue to get sicker every day."

"You will just have to ride this sickness out," the nurse said. "The doctor said you will get better."

I hung up the phone and cried. I knew something was wrong, yet the doctor couldn't help me. She had prescribed medication for nausea, but it only seemed to help for a short time. I lived in a beautiful, century-old, two-story Victorian home, and all of the bedrooms were on the second floor. I was in such pain and so nauseated and alone on this particular day, but the antinausea medication was in the kitchen, which was on the first floor. I was not strong enough to get out of bed to retrieve it. Everyone I knew worked, except one woman who lived in the country, about five miles from my home. I telephoned her, and she came to help me immediately. I explained to her where the medication was located, and she brought it upstairs for me. I was so grateful for her generous spirit that came to my aid that day. When you are in a state of helplessness, your senses sometimes lose direction, and you know you need help, but what to do is a mystery.

The following day, the pain was so severe in my abdomen that I was unable to stand up straight. I called a friend and asked, "Would you please come and help me? I have to go to the doctor, and I'm in severe pain."

He said, "I don't want to go out there and sit all that time. You will have to ask someone else."

I was in utter despair so I drove myself to Urgent Care. I really don't know how I was able to do so, but I believe the angels helped me. In Urgent Care, I waited for the doctor on call to examine me. When the door opened to the examination room, a female physician, with a big smile on her face, entered. She said she had not been scheduled to work in Urgent Care that day, but it was so busy there that she decided to help.

I was relieved to see her; she was very kind and caring.

She said, "Please tell me what you are experiencing."

"I have severe pain in my abdomen, no appetite, I'm nauseated, I've lost thirty-five pounds in the past month, I'm extremely weak, and my hair is falling out."

She reviewed my clinical notes from previous visits and emphatically said, "Oh honey, you are so sick. Let's get you over to the emergency room right away." She quickly found a wheelchair and wheeled me there herself. I was admitted immediately.

After the emergency room doctor examined me and administered several tests, I was admitted to the hospital with a diagnosis of diverticulitis. My urine was the color of bottom-of-the-pot coffee sludge. I was experiencing incredible pain and nausea. At that time, the doctor found I was allergic to penicillin, so the medication administered to me had made me increasingly more nauseated. He administered medication for nausea again, and I remained hospitalized for five days.

Time went by in a blur of doctors, nurses, and blood tests, but the antibiotics began working, and I was finally discharged. My body felt slightly better, but I knew my body; it was still in *dis-ease*. The cause of my illness, that dark ball of energy, was still present.

Several days went by, and my appetite didn't improve. I got weaker once more, and my hair still continued to fall out. Ice cream was all I could eat.

My health continued to decline, and I was barely able to get out of bed any longer. I was not eating, and I felt like I was going to die. Finally, my friend, being extremely concerned, told me, "I am taking you to the emergency room at Mayo Clinic in Rochester." Upon arrival at the ER, the doctor ran several tests and urged me to see an internal medicine physician the following day.

I was discharged and went back home that night. I made an appointment the following morning, and it was yet one more day before I was able to see this specialist. After my specialist at Mayo Clinic examined me, I had more tests and was diagnosed with Graves' disease, an autoimmune disease that affects the thyroid gland. I was considered to be hypothyroid at the time. The plan of care was to administer radioactive iodine to my thyroid gland and inactivate it.

I was quarantined for three days following the procedure, and after a week, I was allowed to return to work. I had to keep my distance from others for that time so they were not exposed to radiation from my body. I lived alone so I requested that others not visit until the time had passed where they were not in danger of exposure. I was also asked to use disposable dishes and dispose of them in a plastic marked bag. I could not be in close proximity to children or to anyone who was pregnant for several weeks. Eventually, I started feeling better. With medication, the Graves' disease is now managed very well.

But this still was not the end. Again, the dark ball of energy continued its journey, wreaking havoc inside my body. It was like a never-ending saga of a hospital soap opera, one that I coined the "Daze of My Life," for that is truly how I felt. My life consisted of doctor visits, medications, and surgeries. Experiencing pain was not unusual. Those who knew me visited with me as I lay in bed, either at home or in the hospital.

The next area it affected was my liver. I became weak again and very tired. I had no enthusiasm or motivation. I finally saw a gastroenterologist at the Mayo Clinic. After several tests, he diagnosed me with hemochromatosis, which is a hereditary liver disease. My mother and father both carried this gene. It was quite unusual for both parents to have passed along the gene, but in my case, it was so. My liver was storing too much iron. Thus began an intense protocol of phlebotomies for five months that extracted a half liter of blood from me every Friday. That was equivalent to a container of store-bought bottled water.

I was rundown and weak from the phlebotomies. Every Friday night, when I went home after having this procedure, my entire body would be incredibly ill. It wasn't that I felt nauseated or fevered, just a sick feeling inside. I would then sleep for two days and return to work on Monday. After a few weeks, I barely knew I was working. I lived in an alternate world of bloodletting and sleeping. I don't know how I kept working, but I did.

Mentally, I could only focus on getting myself to work and only minimally performing my duties because I felt like an empty shell of a person. Emotionally, I was drained. My cup was empty, and I had nothing more to give. I was like a zombie, unable to learn anything new; I functioned on innate abilities, with only previously learned behavior to keep me going. After five months of weekly phlebotomies, I was almost a blank slate. My coworkers couldn't understand what was happening to me. They expected much more from me, but I had nothing more to give. I crept through each day with God's strength to keep me at a minimal functioning level.

When the phlebotomies started to decrease, the dark ball of energy moved to another organ. I was having difficulty breathing and was extremely tired once again. I called my cardiologist early one morning and was able to see him later that morning, a miracle in itself for a Mayo Clinic physician. He examined me but was not sure what was causing my difficulty with breathing. He thought there might be one more possibility, and he requested a CT scan of my lungs.

I drove from the hospital where he had examined me to Mayo Clinic, where I had the scan. After the procedure was completed, I was asked to sit in the waiting room until the radiologist read the scan.

As I waited, my intuition told me that something negative had showed up on the scan. As I was sensing this problem, a radiologist approached me and informed me that he had just finished speaking to my cardiologist, who had requested my immediate return to the hospital for admission. Now quite confused because he didn't tell me the findings of the CT scan, I got to my car and drove back to the hospital.

When I arrived at the hospital, my cardiologist was waiting for me at the entrance; he put me in a wheelchair and admitted me. He was quite distressed when I told him I had driven back to the hospital.

He said, "You have a pulmonary embolism in your left lung and need to have large doses of blood thinners administered right away."

After being hospitalized for a few days, the doctor felt it was safe for me to return home. I was now stabilized on Pradaxa to prevent any further blood clots from forming. Prior to this, I had been on warfarin as a blood thinner, but with so many illnesses and surgeries, I could not be stabilized on that medication. When I was discharged from the hospital, I felt better, and a few days later, I was able to return to work.

Self-defeating thoughts always lingered, and I would pray, "Help me to heal, dear God. I have had enough." My mind traveled its own path of what-ifs, and at times, I would cry as my memories became real once more. Fear was a frequent visitor that swept through me, taking up residency in my mind. When would all of this sickness end? Would it ever end?

Still feeling the dark ball of energy in my body, it next took up residency in my kidneys. During a routine checkup, blood tests revealed an unusual sighting—I was diagnosed with stage 3 kidney disease. This was followed by routine blood tests to measure levels. At this time, I decided to research kidney disease and see if I could heal myself. I changed my diet, my attitude, and my job. I said, "No more stress." I had thought about leaving my position as a case manager for some time, and now, I was sure.

I had remained quite ill during my years of employment with this medical center until my last year in that capacity. I continued to be under a tremendous amount of stress yet again in my workplace, due to a staff shortage, for a variety of reasons.

On the day I decided to terminate my employment, I searched for employment opportunities on the internet that evening and saw a position I thought seemed perfect. I sent a résumé to the Merit System, and there, ironically, was a contact phone number for the manager of the position for which I was applying. I forwarded my résumé to him, along with a cover letter. The next day, I had an email from the manager, and we began conversing about the position.

I gave my notice of resignation to the clinic where I was employed, and at the same time, I developed pneumonia. Again, the dark ball of energy was relentless, never stopping its ravaging effects on my body. My health care involved several specialists from the nation's number-one health care facility in the United States. Each doctor focused on his or her individual specialty. A couple of the diagnoses were hereditary, and others stemmed from my heart condition, as well as stress. When an exorbitant amount of lifetime trauma is experienced, the body takes on its own persona. Past-life trauma accompanies the soul into each life until it is healed. My body, mind, and emotions were products of such trauma, living a life of rejection, abandonment, and fear, as my structural foundation slowly crumbled, yet with a glimmer of light streaming in hope, thus giving me the needed strength to forge forward.

A job interview was scheduled for me during this time, and in spite of having pneumonia, I wanted to interview; I wanted the position. Accompanying the pneumonia was an extreme cough. I decided to accept the interview appointment, pneumonia and all.

Before I went into the building for the interview, I sat in my car and prayed to God to stifle my cough. Blessedly, I walked out of the interview without having coughed, got into my car—and started coughing so hard that I thought I was going to vomit. But oh, how grateful I was that my prayer was answered. The next day, I was offered a position as a psychotherapist at the Human Services Division's mental health clinic in a town thirty miles from where I lived.

I had been a practicing psychotherapist for a few decades and loved working with people.

Corporate therapy had lost its flavor, and I needed to slow the pace; I'd felt like I was really going to die. My friends and sister kept encouraging me to find new employment, and that is just what I did. I loved my new job and the people I worked with—coworkers and clients.

When I saw the kidney specialist again several months later, there was no sign of the stage 3 kidney disease. I cried, and the doctors were amazed!

Life in my new position was relaxing and easygoing. There were three psychotherapists, two psychiatrists, two registered nurses, and the manager of the unit. Each of my coworkers was very focused on delivering the best possible services available to their clients. My manager was a licensed psychologist PhD and was a compassionate man with a wonderful sense of humor. His door was always open to staff, and I found it safe to share with him about my prophetic gifts. He was remarkably in tune with some of the spiritual and metaphysical topics I talked about, and we had a light, fun relationship.

When I came to work in the mornings, I usually went around to each of my coworkers' offices to greet them. I have a bubbly personality, and when I saw my manager, we both immediately smiled. I would say, "Good morning, Matt. You look happy and bright today!"

He would giggle and say, "Good morning, Celeste. How are you today?" Our conversation usually was lighthearted, and then I would disappear into my office to start my day's work.

On one particular day, I came to work feeling happy and looking forward to seeing my clients. Our weekly staff meeting was held, and we all met as a group to discuss clients and their care. As I was discussing an assessment I had completed with a new client, I realized I had lost consciousness momentarily. I looked at my hand that still held the assessment and then at my coworkers and said, "I just blacked out."

They looked at me, shocked, many asking, "What?"

"I just blacked out," I repeated.

My manager immediately asked, "What can I do?"

I was in a surreal sort of reality at the time and answered, "Help me to my office."

My coworkers just stared in confusion. One of the nurses stood up from the table and said, "Come on, Celeste. Let's get you to your office." She and Matt both walked me the short distance, as my office was right next to the conference room. I sat down clearly disoriented.

"Do you want to go to the hospital?" Matt asked.

I said, "I want to call my cardiologist at Mayo Clinic." I called and left a message for him.

The nurse then suggested calling an ambulance, but I did not want to leave work in an ambulance.

Matt then offered to take me to the emergency room, but I said, "I want to go to Mayo Clinic."

The nurse was quite concerned. "I don't think that is a good idea; something more might happen."

Of course, she was right. This blackout had happened as quickly as the first one had. My cognitive abilities were not very keen at that time, so I agreed to let Matt drive me to the ER in town.

After our arrival, I was taken into a room, and I thanked Matt for taking care of me, and he then returned to work. I had tests to examine the functioning of my heart, and after six hours of being there, the attending physician came into my room.

"Your cardiologist at Mayo Clinic has requested that you be taken by ambulance to the Mayo Clinic Hospital for further evaluation."

Once there, I again had several heart-function tests. My heart rate was operating at thirty beats per minute upon admission, which is very low. I had been constantly tired and had been falling asleep quite often for the past couple of weeks, but I thought it was from not getting enough sleep at night. Instead, it was due to my decreased heart rate.

I got a new prescription for my heart medication at the lowest dosage that could be administered, and I started feeling better again. My doctor then had a conversation with me about having a pacemaker implanted.

I told him, "I just can't imagine having an apparatus run my body."

He gently explained, "Your heart rate is functioning improperly, as you know. At certain intervals, there is a 2.5-second lull before its next beat, and that is what leads to the blackouts. It is uncertain as to what the interval is when a blackout occurs; it could be much longer between beats."

"I just need to think about this," I said sadly. "I'll let you know my decision."

I still couldn't fathom having a pacemaker, and when I was discharged, it was without a pacemaker. After this meeting with my cardiologist, I felt strong enough to return to work.

The Return to Work or a Career of Love

> Stairsteps lead to higher outcomes,
> Sometimes winding, sometimes flat,
> Look ahead, the veil does thin.

I was happy to return to a position that allowed my higher self the freedom to operate with such care and love toward others. I felt more peace, knowing that if I had difficulty with my heart again, a solution was available to me. I loved my chosen profession; it never seemed like a "job" to me.

I have always been very dedicated to my profession. Helping others is my passion in this lifetime. I have been honored to engage with each individual and family member, whether aiding to smooth the path to recovery or providing a greater understanding of their situation for them; it also has allowed for greater growth in myself.

My spirituality and enlightenment were beginning a new awakening within me. Many of the clients I worked with were diagnosed with autism. The autism spectrum is quite vast and includes many cognitive and behavioral patterns that make up the clinical diagnosis. I also had several clients who were diagnosed with ADHD (attention deficit disorder/hyperactive type). All of them were children and young adults. I was amazed at what they all had in common.

First of all, they were very high functioning. The next commonality was a tremendous capacity for giving and receiving love. I saw each client on an individual basis and formed a deep connection within spirit. Even though none of them claimed to go to church or have a belief in God, they completely synthesized the same information, even though none of them knew each other and came from different backgrounds.

With spiritual sight, I started seeing them, instead, as a collective of crystal children and star seeds. They all had the characteristics that have been written about such children. They are born from indigo children. From the crystal children will come the rainbow children. All are here on a mission.

The crystal children are here to save the planet. They love being outdoors and have difficulty playing with other children unless they also are crystal children. They have an enormous capacity for love and are very forgiving.

The rainbow children are new souls who will bring peace into the world. The rainbow children are here to heal and rebalance and may be psychic. I believe that is why I understood their journey so well. It is easy for me to identify these children, and I enjoy being around them. There is no judgment, only love, love, love.

I found great joy in working with these clients. Psychiatrists referred them to me because they knew I had the ability to work with them and could see what others could not see. I looked forward to seeing my clients every week. Our sessions were quite unconventional; sometimes I did energy work with them, sometimes qigong, and at times art therapy. They always were a delight, even though the perils of life were harsh for them. Each week, for one hour, they were able to be who they were, glowing and beautiful, and pearls of divine-source energy radiated from their beings. They made progress in difficult areas, such as family, peers, and school, but as I ponder on them, I wonder if they will allow another into their lives with the ability to know who they really are or if I was the only one.

In 2017, I was involved in a car accident; I was rear-ended by another vehicle and diagnosed with a concussion and whiplash. As a result, I was absent from work for two months. During my convalescence, I decided, as I was three months shy of being sixty-seven years old, that it was time to retire from decades of working with the oppressed, abused, and traumatized population I had learned to know well and start exploring the spiritual journey I had longed to live.

My health continued to be well; it had been two years since I was hospitalized with my heart and the conversation about the pacemaker with my cardiologist. One month before my retirement, as I was sitting in my office, a voice spoke to me, and the topics and format for a workshop came flooding in. I was completely engrossed in the information I was receiving and wrote the workshop in three hours that particular morning.

I then called my manager. "I wrote a women's workshop and wondered if I could run it by you."

He came to my office and listened to what I read. "This is wonderful," he said enthusiastically. "It's exactly what others need to hear. Perhaps you should write about how men and women communicate too."

I laughed. "That, Matt, is for another workshop I will develop!"

He was so supportive—a very good and kind man in his profession and a trustworthy friend.

During my career as a psychotherapist, I had been involved with Victims Crisis work and had participated on several community projects pertaining to domestic assault and sexual abuse. My inner self was now telling me to create this workshop to honor all who needed to relearn about their authentic selves and "unlearn" the toxicity that was programmed into their delicate minds.

It was bittersweet, saying goodbye to my clients and coworkers when I left my position. I was ready to release myself from all the trauma and abuse with which I had worked for thirty-five years. My body had been absorbing for long enough the devastation, loneliness, fear, and toxicity that people are conditioned with since prebirth. I wanted and needed a change. Everyone was so accepting and supportive of my next journey in life. I stabilized the transition to other services for my clients and looked forward to retiring to my next adventure.

A decade of illness and disease left much time for me to have in-depth conversations with God. He spoke to me through what I now know to be intuition, feeling, and sensing. Whenever I really needed help, it was provided. I asked the angels for help in many situations. Each time I was hospitalized, I had such loving nurses and doctors.

The spiritual connection that goes on between doctor and patient at that last moment before the mind and body succumb to anesthesia is amazing. Each time before surgery, I would lie on the gurney, waiting to go into the operating room, and tears would run down my cheeks. I would ask the angels to be with me, and sometimes, a loved one's energy would show up, or a doctor would walk by my bed when I was feeling fearful, singing a beautiful love song. I knew it was God.

8
Another New Beginning

God took all the ugliness and messiness
and made it into the most beautiful art.
Always thank Jesus for the Life you have
and the Love he has brought into it.

Retirement was to have its own life, and I was excited to start it. I have been presenting the workshop for the past two years, and it has taken on a life of its own. The workshop is titled "Tune In, Turn On, Tune Up: Women, Empowerment, and Spirituality."

The very first presentation was at the International Conference of Healing Beyond Borders that was held in the fall of 2018. I made slight alterations in the presentation to include men as well, for they too have been victims of life. It is heartbreaking to see all who suffer from the stories told by others that have continued generational toxicity.

Life was feeling so good, and I believed that the work I had been doing to heal myself was freeing me. It was almost Christmas, and the Russian Ballet of *The Nutcracker* was being presented at the Orpheum Theater.

I loved *The Nutcracker*. It had become a holiday tradition for me. I called a friend of mine and asked, "Would you like to attend *The Nutcracker* with me?"

She excitedly said, "I have never seen *The Nutcracker* and would be happy to."

I had previously seen this ballet in San Francisco at the War Memorial Opera House, and it was exquisite at Christmastime with my son and daughter-in-law.

When my friend and I were in the city for the ballet, we had to cross a wide avenue that was very busy with the hustle and bustle of people and traffic. As we crossed, she walked ahead of me and didn't notice that I began to lose my breath and almost blacked out in the middle of the street. Dazed, I kept saying to myself, "You can do it; you can do it; just get to the other side." I felt like I was walking at a snail's pace but finally made it to the curb, frightened and barely able to breathe.

I marvel at the control that the mind has over the body at times. My friend continued to walk ahead of me and had no idea that I wasn't right behind her. As I stood there, afraid and laboring for breath, she turned and saw me. She came back to me and asked, "What are you doing?" I told her what had occurred. She said, "Oh no, are you all right?"

I was getting my breath back at that point and said, "I think so. Let's just get inside the theater."

Still quite weak, I walked about fifty feet to the building. When we got to our seats, I didn't get up until the ballet ended. When we left, I had no problem walking back to the car.

I didn't know what happened but thought it was my heart. This incident frightened me, but I decided to drive home instead of going to a hospital in the city. It was heavily snowing, and it took us two and a half hours to drive home that evening. Usually, it's a one-hour drive, but that night, the roads were covered with snow and ice. Obviously, the journey was quite tense.

The next day, I called my cardiologist and scheduled an appointment. It took a month or so before I could see him, but when we met and I told him what had happened, he said adamantly, "I think it's time for a pacemaker implant, Celeste."

I agreed.

It was spring, and I loved winter being over. There had been so much snow all winter, so being out in nature and feeling the warmth of the sun on my body again delighted me.

The appointment I made for the pacemaker implant could have been done four days earlier, but I told my cardiologist, "I have tickets to see Journey on Friday night, and on Saturday, my dear friend Spirit Light and his band are playing another venue that I want to attend." He laughed and agreed we could wait until the following Tuesday.

When I had the pacemaker surgically implanted, I had to add the delicious fun to the gloomy account of the dark ball of energy. We cannot give all power to the dark.

My path continues. When the pacemaker was implanted, I had restrictions. A line from the pacemaker ran down the interior of the wall of my chest and into my heart. Stabilization of that line had to be secure before I could raise my arm up and over my head, so I had to wear an arm sling to prohibit my unconsciously raising my arm over my head. I also couldn't drive my car for about two weeks after the implant.

A month later, I was able to raise my arm again. Now I have a neat little pocket on the wall of my chest that holds the pacemaker in place, and I am connected to a machine at night that remotely monitors its functioning.

Even though the trials have been many, I never give up hope. Health challenges have accompanied me throughout this life. I have always been an explorer, never staying in the same place once I recognize I can do it differently. I research and practice to make changes. With perseverance and knowledge, I am now healing my soul and body.

The Door Opens Wider

> God does not remove the mountains,
> He teaches us how to climb.

The International Workshop for Healing Beyond Borders was held six weeks after the pacemaker implant. I was still very tired and in the first stage of recovery from the implant. I presented my workshop, and three days later, I boarded a plane for Switzerland with one of my best friends, even though I had very little energy for this beautiful trip.

I was very blessed to meet three people on the tour who also were empaths. We had lovely conversations, and I developed an intimate friendship with one of them.

I also met an empath in Bern, Switzerland—from the moment we saw each other, we connected and had wonderful interactions with each other. It is so comforting to know there are so many in our world who have enlightening gifts!

The most thrilling part of the journey to Switzerland was riding a gondola to the summit of the Matterhorn—miles of glaciers and waterfalls and rock that had the stories embedded from the beginning of this planet. It was one of the most incredible highlights of my life.

Even though my energy was at its lowest point, I was able to spend a day in a miraculous natural outdoor mineral spa and lie in the healing waters for several hours, while the rest of the tour group went off on another adventure. The spa was exactly what I needed to rejuvenate me to go on with the rest of the trip.

Switzerland was amazing, but the glaciers are melting rapidly from global warming and climate change. If we do not make the changes in the mindless polluting of our planet now, we will have completely irreversible damage, and the earth, as we know it, will no longer be. I call for light workers to take action on a daily basis to save our beautiful earth. The ones who are doing the most are the children (perhaps the crystal children). They are begging for the adults of this world to stop destroying it, and the more they beg, the more the earth is being destroyed by those who live in darkness.

The dark ball of energy that dwelt within me is now gone, but I have not been allowed to totally regain my strength. I continue to live this intriguing life that I came here to live, but it is such a challenge at times.

Five months later after the trip, I still felt tired and short of breath. Functioning became harder for me, and I was coughing all the time.

I began spiritual training with my psychic teacher about a year before this incident, and one evening, I asked her, "When I wrote my soul contract before I came here to this earth, this dimension, why did I contract to come into such a sick body? I have been sick my entire life—twenty-four surgeries and other medical problems."

She looked at me very intently and then checked my soul to see if I had the same soul as I'd had before my near-death experience, which I did. She said, "It is not your body that is sick; it is your soul. It came into this body to be healed."

That made perfect sense to me.

I continued feeling tired all the time. The coughing had progressed to the point that it was rare for me not to cough. My shortness of breath and weakness affected my energy level. I became quite listless and sedentary as time progressed.

The apartment I rented had a strange dust that was present since the day I moved in. I talked to the apartment manager several times about this dust and showed her pictures of it.

She spoke to the maintenance man, who retorted, "It is your diffuser that's causing the dust."

I somewhat defensively replied, "The dust was here when I moved in, and I didn't start diffusing for at least six months after that. The dust is inside my kitchen cupboards and drawers—a fine film of the dust covers everything. It is a mixture of white, tan, and scattered brown in color."

When the maintenance man came to my apartment, he said, "I'll start changing your furnace filter every four months. That should take care of it."

I told another person about this problem, and he thought it might be mold coming through my air vents.

Not long after the conversation with my apartment manager, my coughing became so intense that I was admitted to the hospital—I thought I might have problems with my heart again, due to the weakness and shortness of breath. The testing protocol, however, found no problems with my heart.

After a few days of exploration and reading my past records, one of the doctors noted that my lungs had difficulty breathing properly and that there was damage to the endings of my small bronchial tubes. I started nebulizer treatments, and my lungs improved. I was given a home-care regime and was discharged three days later.

My doctor was concerned about the air in my apartment. I told him I was moving in July; at the time, it was the end of December 2018. He suggested I wear a face mask at all times when I was in my apartment, including when I slept.

I had been very prone to bronchitis and pneumonia over the years and had chronic sinusitis. Since that hospitalization, I have used an inhaler for asthma, which I was diagnosed with during my hospital stay, and I irrigate my sinuses daily with a nebulizer solution and a wash for this condition. I have not had any sinus infections for two years and have not had pneumonia for over two years. My asthma improved immensely after I moved from my apartment, and I only use my treatment regime once a day now, instead of twice a day.

My strength started to return quickly, but I continued my daily meditation. I saw new pathways that I was to take that divine-source energy brought to my attention. My mind and spirit work emphatically with each other, reflecting the heart's tears with new beginnings.

After being constantly surrounded by a world of abuse and trauma for several decades in my work life and personal life, I believe that being an empath (one who is very susceptible to other peoples' energies) affected me beyond my knowledge of who I was at the time.

I have attended conferences and workshops that address childhood trauma and the physical dis-ease that the body develops. Many studies have been done on this topic. What I have researched and learned is that my body has only reacted to what it was given—physically, mentally, and emotionally.

As I grew in my spiritual journey, I learned to care for myself and to rid my life of toxic beings and environmental toxicity. My body found joy and health; it found its connection with the collective energies for my higher good, and through that, I found peace.

I am always amazed at how much the human body can endure and that it constantly works to repair itself. Even though I have had a lifetime of sickness and disease, I have experienced more incredible adventures than most people I know. I have seen such beauty and breathtaking sights that the world offers. I have experienced cultures that I didn't know existed and people who have heightened my knowledge of who I *am*.

Harmony of Home

Just as the Universe sings its song, so does my soul breathe music.
The vibration of each note resonates within,
A space without time, a place that is home.

9

Allowing the Love

The Angels Whispered softly
Look, the Caterpillar who from its tightly woven Chrysalis
is emerging a beautifully colored Butterfly

Life has changed miraculously for me. I have been given gifts beyond measure. Yes, the trials were extremely difficult, but each trial taught me a lesson, for lessons are what earth school is about. When the light was allowed to shine, it came forth with such beautiful, radiant color, bringing with its glow the pathway to follow on this journey called life.

As I wrote this memoir, my spirit guides channeled the information through me that was to be included in this book. Spirit guides are those in spirit, not in the flesh, who guide our journeys as human beings. They offer guidance similar to that offered by angels, although spirit guides, at one time, were in human form and now exist in spirit form. They may guide us throughout our entire lives on this planet through spiritual connection. We also may have more than one spirit guide during our lifetimes.

This is my time of healing. My tragic love story has found its way into the divine. I *am* because of who I *am*.

In the next several pages, I will share short memories of those loved ones, all part of my journey, who invested, even for the briefest moment, in who I am today—a spiritual being in a human body, traveling through yet another life.

The following random thoughts are not in any particular order; they are the gifts of many who were chosen to flood my senses at the time of this writing. It is not inclusive of all who have touched my life for healing; these are only some who have held the keys to unlocking the door to my heart for lifetimes past, to enable and allow love to come in. The journey, or, as I have come to recognize, the "release" of my brokenness that plagued my heart, my soul for lifetimes is beginning to find peace.

As long as I can remember, I have felt that my heart was fractured. When I would confide in those I trusted about this feeling, they never recognized it as a truth that I knew about me. This kept me sick, emotionally and physically.

My truth kept crying out, weeping, but no one heard. It was the random love and kindness of others that allowed me to surface, that allowed my heart to be repaired after lifetimes of brokenness. Thoughts of this beautiful space in my chest, which shines the light so readily and eagerly for so much, so many, are infinite in detail.

As a younger woman, I could get down on my knees to honor I *am*. Now, I'm unable to do so, but my heart is honored for the love it contains and the ready willingness it has to pass its unlocking on to others. For that, there are no words, only the welling of what is. My life has now only begun and, in the awareness of what has been given to me, I lovingly share that with you.

Again, the memories are random. I won't attach time periods to them, just what they were and that they are still alive in me—that I *am* who I *am* because of them.

Timelessness

Walk with me for but a bit, that I may meet your soul
A breath now we have been apart, as timeless memories stroll.
I look at you and see me my heart my love doth know,
Rendering falls upon me, as we dance our spirits flow

10

Vignettes of Love

As the veil thins, my heart grows,
seeing in Spirit, the ebb and flow

My Current Love

If only my heart could share the stories of all the lifetimes while in a human body that I have experienced, what a story I could tell. But it is just this one story that rings true at this time; it's the nearest to my memory and reigns in the highest position. A time of endless longings, a soul mate of eternity lived, a time of love and a time of laughter—it all comes back to you, dear lover of my life.

This is a love story of two people who have never met. Five years of writing, calling, supporting each other through great perils, breakups, and, finally, a life-threatening stroke that never allowed for our meeting.

This relationship began easily and sweetly on a social media dating site in 2015. Text messages led to phone calls and more text messages. Sadly, neither of us could find time to meet, for a variety of reasons on both of our parts. We also lived in different areas of the state, which required traveling. As this relationship evolved, it became more difficult—or so I believed at the time—because we had not met. We started having disagreements that led to sadness and discouragement.

Sometimes, life presents obstacles over which we have no control. In 2017, in the time span of one year, I had seven losses. My best male friend died from cancer. I sold my house. I moved into an apartment. I retired from my lifelong career as a psychotherapist. My mother died. My son walked out of my life. Now, after a year and a half, this man, to whom I was growing very close, said he could not handle how emotional I was, and he walked out of my life.

He said, "Celeste, you need to see a psychiatrist or a therapist. You, of all people, should know this."

I became very upset, and the last thread that was holding me together—emotionally, mentally and physically—was fraying quickly. I barely knew what was happening anymore.

I realized I needed help and took his advice. I called a psychotherapist with whom I was familiar and began therapy sessions. I also participated in a Loss and Grief group that covered all losses, and I intently worked on my homework assignments. I started feeling stronger after a couple of months, and my focus improved greatly, as well as my general outlook on life. Being an incredibly resilient woman, I decided it was time to start living my life again.

It had been six months since Trey had said his last words to me. During these six months, I felt his warm energy swirling around me every day. Sometimes, it was so intense that I was incapable of continuing the task at hand. My body became immobile, and I would speak to him through the universe, through divine-source energy, to tone down his thoughts of me because I couldn't function. Slowly, the energy would decrease, and I would be able to continue what I was doing.

It was February 2018, about 12:20 a.m., and I was watching a movie on TV. Life had started settling a bit. I was involved in completing plans to present a workshop I had written at an international conference. As I looked down at my phone, I saw his name. Every ounce of adrenaline that rushed in drained faster. I felt like an oozing pile of melting emotions that had finally thawed and had now turned into a current of—*what*? I kept looking at the name on the phone. After some time, I captured enough courage to open the text.

There it was, from the heart—a message of declared love? Loneliness? What? What? It read:

> When I look at you, Celeste, I am in love with all of you. I told you that you
> were so emotional with your feelings that you scared me away. The truth is,
> that is one of the many things about you I love so much; you are ready to
> give all of yourself and enjoy being in love.

Having time to wonder why I am still looking for a woman just like you, it's not that you scared me away from you, the more intense you became with wanting me; it's that I was getting cold feet and scared to let myself go completely with loving you immensely.

Which is exactly what I am looking and want with a beautiful angel as you in my life. Every time I look at your pictures, all that I can think of is how much you excite me, for you to be close to me, in my arms and making love to me in every way I crave to exhaust myself, loving you freely. You always make my heart skip a beat when I see your pictures, beautiful angel.

I was speechless. I sat there for the next four hours, reading that message over and over again, crying. I didn't know what to do. Part of me was happy; the other part experienced all the sadness of six months ago all over again. What to do? I talked to my best friend about the message and then went to sleep for a few hours. When I awoke the next afternoon, I agreed to talk with him. After that conversation, I decided to become involved again.

Trey promised, "I will never do this again." And I believed him.

Our relationship was much more open after the separation, and Trey and I spent hours on the phone, talking about our lives and things we enjoyed. I was growing closer to him and loved the connection we had.

We did not get to meet at this time because I had influenza twice during the winter and spring and was too sick to do so. Summer came, and he was busy again. I wanted to meet, but it did not happen. I found myself feeling discouraged again. I was open with what I was looking for in a relationship—companionship, honesty, love; one day, I would like to get married again. I asked, "Are we on the same wave?"

He lovingly answered yes.

Then one day, Trey said softly, "Please have patience with me, Celeste."

I agreed. I felt that if we had met before the six-month separation, we would not have been able to get the relationship back together. Neither of us was capable of functioning in a relationship. We both were dealing with emotional demons, and at times, I felt very needy and didn't like myself having that persona.

Being a strong, professional woman who recently had recovered from a year of "layered" loss and grief (this term is used when several losses occur in a short time span), devastation, and turmoil. I could see now how Trey and I interacted together. I was trying to be cognizant of that as we moved forward.

One month before my sixty-eighth birthday in September, we were planning to meet. We usually said good night to each other before going to sleep, and on this particular evening, I received a text message from him that read, "Good night, beautiful angel."

I did not hear a word from him again for almost a month and a half. Then, one evening in mid-October, a text came in from Trey: "In recovery. Stroke."

I cried so hard that night. I didn't know if I would lose him.

As he became stronger, I heard from him more often. Then one day, he wrote, "My doctor visited today and commented, 'I'm surprised you lived. You were in such bad shape.'"

I didn't know what to do, and honestly, I still don't. He experienced a hemorrhagic stroke, which affected his vocal cords. When we had phone conversations, his voice was weak, and he had slight difficulty with enunciating some syllables.

What a miracle his life has been. Trey's left side was affected, so walking has been quite a challenge for him. I believe God saved his life for a reason, and I am so excited to witness what that reason will be. Maybe God just knew that I still needed him or that we needed each other.

I've written about the times that I remember with this man I almost lost, our loving experiences together, and the only way I could be part of his life at the time.

The twinkling smile of your eyes, the deepness of eternity looking at me. The fullness of your lips as they curve to complete what your eyes began. We have been together for so long, yet only in the blink of an eye, and it is over, to come back yet again, to be the endless love story we started so long ago.

So many nights I thought of you as I sat in silence, with only my heart to tease my mind, longing for the time when I may see you again. The darkness of your skin, shimmering in the sunlight as it played in the garden. You sent me so many pictures, and I saw you living your life. Oh, how the morning glories and roses loved you as you gently manicured each one, only to have them thank you with their brilliant magnificence. You took timeless care of what you had created—a garden of Eden, in a sense—to find your peace and tranquility.

The birds happily sang as they feasted on the deliciousness of the treats you left for them each day. You cared so much for these small, winged beauties and awaited their return each spring. You sent videos of the birds at their feeders and bathing in the pond you built, with the fountain in its center.

Fondly, you sent colorful pictures to me of an array of butterflies, busy little bees, and other insects that lived in the garden. You found such delight in capturing their beauty and passing the excitement on to me. And as I viewed each of the lovely photos, I not only saw what you were experiencing, but I also saw the warmth in your heart for the delicate plants and insects that made up the life you were living. You shared yourself with me every day so that I could see life through your eyes.

At times, especially in the colder months, you invited me into your world indoors. I had the opportunity to see you creating who you were, in the rooms you were working on, as our fondness for each other grew.

I enjoyed being a part of all that you did. You always were so serious when looking for new additions to your surroundings, sharing pictures of curtains and duvets to enhance your subtle delights.

As you created, you were creating me—all of what I loved and enjoyed was the palette from which you painted.

At times, you would call when you were out, rummaging through thrift shops. Our excursions were always a treat! Busily, you took pictures, sending them to me as you happily scoured through the endless piles—"What do you think of this?" I would chuckle, and you would continue shopping. If you found an item that really caught your fancy, you were so excited and told me every detail. "Isn't this lovely? Look at the little roses on this duvet." Or if you were shopping for appliances, you would send a picture, asking, "Do you like this refrigerator?" and then describe it to me. I loved every minute of the hours we spent as you shared your treasures with me. Your joy and innocence were inspiring as I watched and listened to your busyness of being you.

I remember one day when you asked me, while we were on the phone, "Do you know how to change a tire?" I thought it funny that you would ask such a question, but you said, "I like a woman who knows how to do lots of things."

I just laughed. "Yes, I have changed a few in my lifetime!"

Working on your car or truck or building an area in the kitchen for your washer and dryer, painting, laying carpet—it didn't matter; it was time that we spent together through pictures and phone calls, as I got to know who you were. When you put granite blocks on the walls in the laundry area, you took pictures as you talked to me about it. I have several pictures of that laundry area now! You built it from a closet off the kitchen. I was so impressed. As you brought me in closer, I became closer—until now, not being able to imagine life without you.

And it was not only you who was inviting me into the life you lived. I also continued to create and, by doing so, I invited you into the life that was me. When I created my workshop, you were so supportive. The day I was called about presenting my workshop at the international conference, we were on the phone together. A beep came in, and I excitedly blurted out, "Oh my gosh! Colorado is calling. I will call you back." When I called you back, I joyfully shouted, "My proposal has been accepted!" We were both so excited!

Then you added, "Make that title your own now." I did.

All of my excitement became what you knew me to be. All of the travels to different parts of the country or overseas—sometimes you were with me through pictures and videos, and at others, you were off somewhere else but always knew of my travels.

My spiritual growth has been amazing, and my having the ability to feel you through spirit has been what has most sincerely kept us together. I feel you swirling around me, and my heart longs for you. You also became connected to me and saw the strong yet sensitive, feeling woman that I am.

And the growth we have both done has been amazing, learning how to be with each other, how to react to each other, and to care about each other. As we allowed each other in, we have discovered more about who we are. There is so much more to learn. I remember writing to you, "Our foundation is built strong, and it is not of sand and twigs but of mortar and emotion. I have come to see you as the man I care so deeply for, the one who brings a smile to my face in the morning and the one who turns off the lamp at night, as I hold you in my dreams and pray for us, as I gently flow into slumber."

Allowing you into the loving cradle of my heart sometimes brought me to tears as we grew together. Sometimes, you would send me a text message so full of love and caring that I would sit back in my chair and feel your energy swirl around me, at times so entwined that I could hardly breathe. Sometimes, this would last for several minutes. Softly, I once told you, "The sadness has always been that, with all that we have shared, we have not yet looked into each other's eyes or felt the warm tenderness of each other's touch." Your voice would become quiet when I would talk like that. I felt what you were not saying.

The days go by so quickly, and as you are hidden from me, I feel the heaviness of the separateness in the physical that lingers on for us. When you had your stroke, I felt as if my world came crashing down upon me. You were so sick and didn't want me to see you the way you were. You said, after you were able to text and call again, "Please respect me with this. I want to meet you at my best." Oh, how I wished you would not keep me away from the most challenging experience of our lives together thus far, but there was no budging you.

As I think about you, I am taken each time to my heart, to feeling the breath I breathe, the beauty of your soul, and I see us in an enchantingly peaceful place in my mind, hearing the music that our beings create.

The laughter we had together, the funny little songs you would sing, and the silly little sounds you make has me feeling so delicious in being part of us. I remember laughing so hard at your singing one day that all I could do was make noises. "Stop! I can't breathe!" Then you sent the song to me from YouTube!

Now, as day ends and night comes to a close, I miss you in the depth of my soul. You are part of us, and that is what I hang on to. Once more, I see your twinkling eyes and loving smile that turns my heart into a beautiful pink lantern and wait to show you the way to me. In the background, a familiar song plays, one that you sent to me long ago and asked, quite adamantly, "What do you think of this music?"

I softly whispered, "It reminds me of us—"How, When, Where" by Cleo Laine/Pachelbel, Canon in D major.

Your Secret Garden

You are, by far, my love, the fairest of flowers that grow in your garden,
For it is your smile that brings forth the sunshine, opening each radiant petal.
Blossoms unfolding to release a fragrance of hope,

Bringing forth once more the splash of color, of beauty, an artist's palette born,

From my loved one's intricate vision
A landscape now adorned.

And the shadows came into the Light
And there I was

My College Sweetheart

This young man, of whom I will so adoringly speak, and I met one evening with a friend of mine, who coincidentally was also a friend of his. My friend invited me to accompany him to hear a very popular blues band in the metro area that night. As we walked through the doorway of the venue, I was immediately pulled into the groove of the music. As we stood there, dancing and watching the band, I asked curiously, "Do you know the drummer?"

He laughed. "Yes, he lives near me. We went to high school together."

When the band took a break, the drummer walked over to us, and my friend said, "Hey Daniel, this is my friend Celeste!"

We smiled at each other, and I was smitten at first sight. We started to talk, and I found him somewhat shy and demure. I could tell he had a very gentle spirit, and upon our meeting, I was assured that he did indeed carry a loving light within him.

At the end of the evening, after periodic conversation during each break, Daniel said, "Would you mind if I called you?"

I happily wrote down my phone number and said, "I look forward to talking with you again."

He and my friend hugged, and we left the concert. My friend and I chattered away like squirrels on the way home. I asked, "Is Daniel as nice as he seems to be? Does he have a girlfriend? Where does he live?" Typical nineteen-year-old conversation.

Daniel had shoulder-length dark-blond hair, deep blue eyes, and a medium-size frame; he was quite handsome. I was excited to hear from him again. After arriving home that night, my phone rang, and it was Daniel.

He said, "I would like to get to know you better. I hope it isn't too late for conversation."

I thought, *Are you kidding? Of course it's not too late.*

We spoke for two or three hours that night. Daniel called almost every night after that, and we grew quite fond of each other. He lived about forty minutes from me, and whenever he could use his mother's car, he would come to see me. I was in my first year of college at the time, and life was fun and exciting. When Daniel called, our conversations were usually very deep, and we would talk for hours.

One winter's evening, Daniel came knocking at my door. "Are you ready?"

We were going out for a cozy dinner at a little diner just up the street from where I lived. As he came through the door, my eyes twinkled at seeing him. I was wearing one of my best dresses, with shoes to match, along with my warm winter coat, as it was quite cold in the Midwest during the winter.

I was so excited to start yet another new journey with him. As I hurried out onto the landing and took my first step, my feet slid on the ice, and I slid down the four steps on my behind to the sidewalk. "Ahhhh!" I said, as I looked up and saw him standing next to me. He bent down, held out his hand, and helped me up. He dusted me off with his hand and then, gently, with a heart filled with love, asked, "Are you hurt? Do you need anything?

I said no and shyly looked at him. I think I expected him to laugh and leave. I don't know why I had those thoughts, probably because I was so embarrassed. He then took my hand and asked, "Are you all right to go to dinner, Celeste?"

I said yes, and off we went. Daniel was so polite and considerate, and I liked him.

Layers

Removing a layer of costume,
Exposing yet another view of me,
Slowly unfolding, another light shines,
I know you are seeing me as I am each time,
More wonderment, more wondering, more wonderful.

My Horse and My Dog

These are memories of my two best friends as a young adolescent—my horse, Buck, who was a buckskin quarter horse, and my dog, Duke, who was a stately black-and-gold German shepherd. I loved them so much and spent most of my time with them. We rode the countryside and traveled many journeys together.

I belonged to a saddle club, and we would spend weekends, occasionally during the summer, with our horses trucked in semis to state parks or other incredible areas in the Midwest for trail rides. One day, as I sat high in the saddle, I leaned over my horse's neck and put my arms around him. I felt the strength of his strong body that had carried me so many miles during our time together. Duke ran beside us, if we didn't travel too far, as a trusty companion. They were not only my two best friends but also my escape from the toxicity of the parental unit with whom I occasionally lived.

Buck was a strong, muscular horse, and my aunt taught me how to train him for barrel races and to show him in horse shows. I had riding outfits, with cowboy boots and cowboy hats to match. I loved showing my horse. Although he did not talk, I certainly said plenty to him. I would tell him, "You are such a good boy," or "You did really great, Buck." He was a savior in my life, and he didn't even know it.

My dog, Duke, was by my side all the time when I stayed at my mother's in the country. He was not allowed in the house, but when no one was home, I would let him in, and we'd watch TV together, have snacks, and play around. One day when I was gone, my mother told me that Duke got in the house and would not leave.

She said, "I tried talking nice to him, hollered at him, and he wouldn't budge." My mother was quite irritated at this time. "Finally, I was able to coax him out the door with a pound of hamburger." Then she glared at me. "Do you let that dog in this house when we are gone?"

I lied and said no.

But honestly, many nights Duke would be in my bedroom, having jumped in through the window, and I'd lie on my bed, talking to him and putting my arm around him as he'd rest his head on the side of the bed. He was a faithful companion and loved me when those I lived with couldn't even love themselves, let alone a child.

Duke did not like my mother or my stepdad and was not good at following their commands. When I was with my mother, I rode the school bus to school. Duke would always wait for the bus with me and would be waiting at the end of the day for the bus. I'm sure he heard its unique sound coming down the tar road we lived on.

Then one day, as I arrived home on the school bus, I was greeted by devastating news. Duke, who had been standing on the side of the road, waiting for the bus, had been hit and killed by a car. I was consumed with loss and ran to the barn to be with Buck. My stepfather sadly said, "I'm taking his body to bury it." He was buried at the end of our pasture. I cried so hard. I had lost one of my best friends. I visited his grave frequently and mourned his death.

The connection between animals and humans is sometimes richer than most human connections. Their unconditional love, given so freely, creates a lasting bond. Even with the writing of this, I still feel their companionship in my life.

A Child Giving Birth to a Child

When I was sixteen, I lay in labor, fearfully awaiting the birth of my first son. My grandmother sat patiently at my hospital bedside so I wasn't alone. I had no knowledge of what giving birth entailed and had not been given any education in that regard. There I was, a child, waiting to give birth to a child. The contractions were incredibly intense (if you have ever had hard labor in childbirth, you know what *intense* is). I had no other thoughts except what was happening in that very moment—mindfulness in the extreme, right there, right now, period. I liken it to an out-of-body experience that just you and your feelings will ever know.

I was crying and pleading for help. I experienced intense labor for twenty-four hours, and my beautiful grandmother stayed by my bedside, holding my hand and loving me more with each contraction. The contractions were almost constant, and she soothingly talked to me, but I could feel her pain for me. Even though I faintly heard her words, I could feel her, and the unconditional love she had for me held strong. She would be there, no matter what. She was there because she wanted to be.

A Sense of Security (Second Husband)

It was a humid July evening—the weather felt quite unstable—and I was sitting in a booth with my boyfriend Ben, enjoying pizza at a local establishment. Ben was a tall man, six foot five, with shoulder-length black hair, dark-brown eyes, and a large frame. It had been very hot and humid all day, and frequently, with that type of humidity, came intense storms in our part of the upper Midwest. Ben and I enjoyed conversing with each other, and we talked about many subjects at age twenty-seven. I was a dreamer, and my ideas conjoined with his. He was funny and always had me laughing. His favorite line was, "I've been down so long it looks like up." Although on one level, it was a rather funny comment, it also had depth for my analytical mind, a feeling I was familiar with.

As we sat and talked, a sudden shrill siren startled me—it warned that a funnel cloud had been sighted and the probability of a tornado approaching. I had always been terrified of tornadoes. Ben took my hand as he scanned the restaurant. Then he looked into my eyes, softly yet strongly, and said, "Don't worry. I will take care of you." I knew he would. Several months later, I married him because he'd said he would take care of me that night.

Near-Death Experience

In 1991, I decided to travel to my best friend's college graduation. She had earned her master's degree in social work, and I was so proud of her. It was a beautiful, warm, sunny spring day, and I was in the company of John, my boyfriend of three years. After traveling for several hours, it was getting dark, so I asked, "Should we spend the evening in this fun little tourist town up ahead?"

John happily said, "Sure, that sounds great!"

This area was known for its variety of activities, and we took advantage of this opportunity.

During dinner that night, I suddenly became incredibly tired and could not stay awake. John kept asking me, "Are you all right?"

"I'm just so tired," I answered. I don't even remember eating my food. We left the restaurant and returned to our motel room. I don't remember falling asleep.

The next morning, the unbelievable happened. I became very ill in six short hours and almost died.

Several weeks later, I was in an intensive care unit of a hospital far from home, in another midwestern state. John sat at my bedside; he recently had moved out of my home. He was there on that particular weekend as a last effort to see if our relationship could be saved. John was an alcoholic, and his habitual relapsing had torn the relationship apart. I was in recovery, and it was not working for me with him drinking. As he watched me, I slowly rejoined this world, after coming back from death. He peered at me over the top of the bed rail.

The nurse had just removed my feeding tubes, after a month of that being my major source of nourishment, and she asked, "What would you like to eat?"

I enthusiastically answered, "Ice cream!" During all the days that turned into weeks, I had stared up at those beautifully colored bags of whatever was in them, reminding me of sweet, yummy ice cream. Now the time had come; I was going to have ice cream.

When the ice cream arrived, John stood next to my bed, resting his arm on the bed rail, his long blond hair teasing his face. He smiled down at me with hope as he put a bit of ice cream on the tip of a spoon and gently slid it into my mouth. I'm not sure which one of us was more excited. I was smacking my lips and making that "yum-yum" sound as I tasted its cold sweetness. I looked up at him, and he had the biggest smile on his face, as if he had just fed a baby its first food.

He then asked, "Is that good, Wheatie?" That was his pet name for me; he said I had hair the color of wheat.

I happily said, "Oh yes, more, more." I smiled and giggled as I watched him dip the spoon again in all that sweet, yummy ice cream. Beaming now, I looked in his eyes and whispered, "Thank you, John."

A Peaceful Departure

After my near-death experience at the age of forty-two, I had the honor of sharing my miraculous story at my church and other venues about crossing over and being in the spirit realm. Now, my travels had me sitting at the bedside of a frightened, beautiful, sixteen-year-old girl in an intensive care unit at a major hospital. I had met her at an AA meeting a couple of years prior to this. One of her family members had told me she was in the hospital and had asked that I visit her.

As I sat with her and held her hand, quietly she asked, "What is it like when we die?" She had cancer and was near the end. She knew of my near-death experience.

With love in my heart, I answered, "I did not have an awareness of a body, yet my consciousness was in a wonderful place. There was such exquisite beauty; magical pastel gardens provided a sweet, airy fragrance, and there was a warm peace in this place, a sense of freedom and unconditional love."

Her soft brown eyes gazed up at me, and she said innocently, "I am not afraid now."

As I looked at her frail body and her shiny bald head, there was a brightness, a calmness, a peace. That scene is branded in my memory. She died shortly after that. She gave me a part of herself that day, which remains with me now.

Educational Malfunction

One stressful afternoon, as I worked intensively on my clinical research paper, my all-important master's thesis, my computer stopped functioning. All of the work I had done vanished with the death of this machine! There was no backup. I had just begun working on the computer and knew very little about the machine—only how to turn it on. I was beside myself with fear, anger, and helplessness. I didn't know what to do. I felt like I had failed. I telephoned my fiancé's mother and gave her the devastating details about the incident as my tears fell. She lovingly told me she had just purchased a computer and said if I came over, I could use it for as long as I needed or until my research paper was completed.

When I arrived, she had it ready for me. I thanked her profusely and took it home. When my thesis was finished and bound, one of the dedications on the first page was to her for her kind, considerate generosity with the finishing of my project.

A Kindly Gesture

As I started to step from the bus, I felt a hand take mine, gently guiding me to the ground. A man I did not know stood there with a smile. I thanked him and walked away.

Heartfelt Love

When I was working as an area director of an adoption agency, I was honored to have a group of prospective adoptive parents, sitting at tables in a U-shape form, in a facility that was about changing lives. They had just been handed manila envelopes that contained pictures and important information about the child/children they were strongly considering adopting. Prior to this, they had only seen pictures on paper copied from a computer screen.

I could see the hope and anticipation in their eyes as they carefully opened their envelopes, almost ceasing to breathe. I focused on one woman who had gone through all the adoption studies and classes and was so excited with her decision to move forward. She removed the material from the envelope, and there before her were the pictures of her most cherished children. Tears came to her eyes as her heart melted. She fell in love at that moment, and so did I.

It is our spirits that first connect.

Speaking from the Heart

I had the honor of being the speaker at a twelve-step meeting one evening, held at a halfway house for chemically dependent residents; it was always quite a large meeting. My secretary accompanied me that evening. She was such a joy to be around, a bubbly and happy soul. Usually, the speaker was allocated approximately forty-five to fifty minutes. I had been at the podium for about forty-five minutes and was closing my story.

As I stepped away from the podium, I felt quite weak; it was as if I'd used up all the energy that my heart held as I'd shared the story of my recovery from drugs and alcohol. I was happy to put my hand on the railing that led down the steps and get back to my table.

I collapsed into my chair and said, "Boy, am I glad they have that railing there because I would not have made it back here without it!"

My secretary looked at me, surprised, and said, "What railing? There's no railing there."

I looked and, astonishingly, there was not.

Education and Clairvoyance

In 1999, I was involved in a field practicum as part of the master's program in social work that I was completing. A local human services agency had agreed to supervise me and I was assigned three clients on my caseload. I had spent the day with a client who had been assigned to me while I was doing the field practicum. It was quite an unusual day with him. This client had experienced several self-injurious behaviors and had taken me into his confidence. I felt honored to have this practitioner/client relationship.

As I sat across from my client, I thanked him for sharing his being with me. I said, "Now that I know, you are not alone in there. The door has been opened, and the light can come in, if you choose to allow it."

The following day, I met with my supervisor to review the previous day's events and what I had learned that day. I explained to my supervisor, "This client allowed me to see into his soul during the visit and to experience the darkness, the pain, the fear, and loneliness he lives with on a daily basis. I don't know how long I was in his subconscious mind, just that it was light outside when we started, and when I came out of that place in his mind, it was dark outside."

My supervisor looked at me in wonder and with respect. "I will never hire you as a county social worker," he said. "You have a much greater gift. Now go out and use it!"

I didn't understand what he meant at the time, but I have come to know the gift he handed to me that day—his trust in what I was and what I would become. He saw it long before I could.

Hope Amid Uncertainty

There was great dysfunction in my work center, and I was about to quit my job. I was torn between the clients and the harshness in the work environment. I called my friend, who was a county corrections manager, and he came right over.

"You are worth more than what is happening here," he said. Then, he looked me in the eye. "It's OK. You can do whatever you set your mind to."

I quit. I knew he was right

Age Has No Barrier in Kind Conversation

I was basking in the sun one beautiful, warm afternoon on a southern Mexico beach, enjoying the lively music in the background, when a tall young man with blue eyes and short blond hair walked up and sat down next to me. He seemed quite friendly. We were surrounded by college spring-breakers, and I asked, "How old are you?"

He smiled. "I'm twenty-five."

After an afternoon of lengthy and spirited discussions and light-hearted fun, I looked at him and said, "Why is it—"

"Why is it," he interrupted, "that a young man of twenty-five is spending all this time with an older woman, instead of looking at all the girls my age?" He'd taken the words from my mouth. As I looked at him intently, he said, "Because the girls my age have nothing to talk about. They just giggle and try to look cute. You're interesting, and I enjoy your company."

I was speechless, except to say thank you. I was thirty-nine at the time.

We spent an amazing afternoon, enjoying interesting conversation and laughter that day.

Friends, Music, and Healing

As I lay in the hospital bed, totally paralyzed after my near-death experience but able to speak, I learned that a dear friend and his band were to be guests on a famous late-night talk show in New York that evening and would perform one of their new songs. I was so excited. I asked my nurse to position my bed directly in front of the TV that was hanging on the wall so I could see the screen well.

As I watched him walk out onto the stage, and the late-night host kept repeating his name, tears welled up inside me for my beloved friend. In my mind, I said, "Yeah, dear one, if only you could see your friend Celeste, lying here in this hospital bed."

The first time I was able to move my hand was as I watched him, and I could feel his energetic love for me.

Too Much Fun

I was walking through a busy department store one wintry evening with my best friend and felt my light shining. I tried on a variety of sunglasses with silly, unusual frames and took pictures of myself, laughing and loving being in the moment. I looked up from my gaiety and noticed several people had stopped and were laughing at the fun I was having. They too found their inner children that evening, and we all shared the laughter.

Rehab Angel

For almost three years, I had been working with vocational rehabilitation services after being diagnosed as 100 percent disabled from a motorcycle accident that caused extensive injury to my lower back. This service had furnished the financial funding for me to go back to college to get my associate of applied science and associate of arts degrees.

I was graduating with a 3.8 GPA. I had been on a career path in college as a human care specialist, but now, I was faced with what was to happen next. My vocational rehabilitation counselor and I discussed my future. He was very supportive of my continuing my education for two more years and to earn my bachelor of science degree in social work.

He was a very easygoing man in his mid-fifties, with short, sandy-colored hair; a soft, kind voice; and eyeglasses that slid down his nose every few minutes. He had taken great interest in my life due to my disability and my enthusiasm about college. We had many enlightening conversations during our three years together. I was so grateful for his support in my life.

What I knew about myself at the time was that I was afraid of success, and I was afraid of failure.

As we sat across from each other, he spoke intently. "Celeste, I want you to take all the minuses in your life and turn them into pluses."

From that day forward, I did.

Healing on Christmas Eve

On Christmas Eve 1986, my son and I attended a church service in our community. As I've mentioned, I had been involved in a seriously debilitating motorcycle accident and had spent four of the past five years in a wheelchair, in and out of hospitals, and in a body cast. Most recently, I'd had surgery for three crushed discs in my lower back and a laminectomy. I was able to walk but continued to experience significant pain. I could only sit on hard, straight furniture. As we sat that night on the ergonomically challenged wooden pew, the pastor announced that there were five faith healers at the service that evening, and after the service, those in the congregation who wished to do so could go down to the altar and be prayed over for healing.

My son was thirteen at the time and had always had so much faith. He looked at me as we got up from the pew and slowly edged our way to the aisle. "Mom, what are you going to do?"

Surprised, I said, "I don't know."

I immediately stepped from the row and went to the altar without thought.

As I knelt at the altar, the faith healers approached me and asked, "What can we help you with?"

I shyly answered, "Four years ago, I was involved in a motorcycle accident. I had three crushed discs in my back." I had not planned on telling them about my early recovery—six months from drugs and alcohol—but without hesitation, I added, "I am also a recovering alcoholic and drug addict of six months." I shared all of this information with the healers in what seemed like a minute in time. They anointed me with oil and started speaking in tongues. The only thing I remember from that point on was experiencing an overwhelming surge, like a lightning bolt entering the top of my head, traveling down my spine, and shooting out the end of my tailbone.

When I opened my eyes, I was standing again, and several women from the church had circled around me, praising God and giving thanks for what they had witnessed. I do not know what they saw, only what I felt, and I truly was infused by the energy of God. I stood there breathing pure, fresh air, as if I was in a forest by a gently flowing brook. I knew that I was filled with the Holy Spirit.

That night, my son and I went home and sat in front of our Christmas tree on the couch, which I had not been able to do for four years. We cried because of the healing I had received. All the pain was gone, and I was free!

If Today Were the Only Day That I Had

If today were the only day that I had, I would wish to have everyone I have ever loved in my life, who has created an impact in my life for its highest good, who has held my hand as the tears came forth, who cried because of the pain my body experienced or my heart felt, who was a patient teacher, watching my life unfold, who has stretched out their hands and pulled me up, who rejoiced at even the smallest of discoveries in my childlike eyes, who touched my life with only a smile or laughed with me until tears streamed, who was before me and actually saw *me*, those who have experienced my kiss or felt my touch, I'd put them into an endless circle that surrounds all that is. I would go to each one and feel the silence of overwhelming love that has been created within who I am. This, indeed, would take yet another lifetime.

My Gift as a Caregiver

At the age of forty-three, I was employed as Director of Social Services in a rural health care facility. I loved it and became quite involved in the daily activity of helping those in the facility experience just a bit of dignity and worth, as their days were limited. One such day, I was called to the bedside of a gentle woman who had been a joy in my days at this facility. She told me she was going to the hospital and was waiting for the ambulance to come for her.

As I looked at her, a sadness filled my heart. I knew I would not see this lovely woman again. I took her hand and said, "Would you like me to read to you from the Holy Bible?"

She replied, "I would like that."

I told her I was going to read a scripture that I'd found most comforting when I was beginning life anew after my near-death experience. I opened the Bible to Psalms 103 and read the first four verses:

Bless the Lord, O my soul: and all that is within me, bless his holy name.

Bless the Lord, O my soul, and forget not all his benefits:

Who forgiveth all thine iniquities; who healeth all thy diseases;

Who redeemeth thy life from destruction; who crowneth thee with lovingkindness and tender mercies

The ambulance crew then walked into the room with the stretcher for her. We said our goodbyes to each other and hugged, and I felt the wasting of her frail, aged body in my arms. I squeezed her hand as she was strapped on the gurney and watched as they wheeled her out of the building. I said, "I'll be seeing you."

I knew I would never see Clara again, at least not in this lifetime. I felt the loss beginning to happen. A few days later, I was told of her death and when her funeral was scheduled. I asked the director of nursing if I could attend the funeral, and she thought that was a good plan.

As I sat in the church pew that day, with my heart full of sadness for my loss of this insightful, beautiful stranger I had come to call my friend, the pastor started the service. I was alone, and as the pastor spoke of this beautiful woman, my mind traveled as the conversations we'd had, and they wove in and out of the service.

As he finished his eulogy, he told the congregation that the first Bible reading for the day would be Psalm 103. I heard myself gasp as the tears found life yet again, and I knew my dear Clara was watching over me.

The Assistance from an Angel

I recently had secured employment with a chemical-dependency treatment program in a small town, about thirty-five miles from where I was living. After being in my new position for about a month, I decided to move. I liked the new town and was able to rent a very nice duplex about four blocks from where I worked. My birthday was my moving day. I had asked several friends and previous coworkers to help with the move. I rented a U-Haul truck, and on moving day, one of my friends said, "I will pick up the truck for you."

When he returned, the people I had asked to help, about a dozen of them, all showed up. This dear friend then orchestrated the packing of the truck and drove the truck to my new home. When we arrived, there were about twenty men and women waiting to greet me, and they unloaded the truck and helped set up the bed frames. When everyone was gone, my friend and I went to a pizza shop and celebrated my birthday. As I was quite worn out, he graciously offered to drive the truck back to the U-Haul store for me. "You just get some rest," he said.

I thanked him for his hard work and selfless kindness. He drove away on the thirty-five-mile return journey. That was the last time we saw each other. There was no particular reason; we just didn't. He called once to see how I was doing, and that was our last phone call. We had known each other for a couple of years before that, and he was a wonderful friend. I had blessing upon blessing with that move. Those friends cannot imagine the impact they had on my life that day.

Being Honored by My College Professor

The day had finally arrived, and I was now walking out onto the stage of a very large auditorium, still reeling in disbelief that I had earned the master of social work degree for which I had worked so hard and diligently. I noticed the faculty all lined up and sitting in chairs on the stage. They stood up as we students made our way to the podium to receive our degrees. As I passed my instructors, I noticed my most dedicated professor standing there. As I walked closer, he turned, looked into my eyes, and placed his hands together in front of his chest in honor of me and my accomplishment. Even though it felt surreal, this was really happening.

Heavenly Transition to Continue Her Work

She called me every day on the phone for at least a year—an exquisite soul in her late eighties. She was always helping others and believed that was her calling on earth. We met at a difficult time of my life, and she took me under her wing. My son's father had a life-threatening health problem, and she said she would pray for him several times every day until he was cured. I believed her. Each day when she called, the first thing she wanted to know was how he was doing. She gave so much strength and unconditional love to us both. I looked forward to her calls and could talk to her about anything. She was pure love in motion.

One day, the phone did not ring, and I knew something was wrong. I tried to call her several times, but no one answered. Two days passed, and my phone rang. It was my mother. She said, "I just wanted to tell you that Sara was found dead in her bed this morning."

I felt numb and had nothing to say to my mother. She knew of Sara, as they both attended the same church. I hung up the phone and prayed. "Thank you, God, for this message about Sara. I will miss her so much. Take good care of her, Lord."

I cried for the loss of her in my life; my son's father cried for her in his heart. I knew that there was just too much for her to do, and in order to do more, she had to leave her human body and join source energy in its highest form.

Three years later, my son's father was healed from his disease. Thank you, my dear friend, for your connection with Most High and with me.

Making Amends in My Recovery

My first husband, whom I divorced in 1976, came to visit several years later after I invited him to do so. We'd had a tumultuous marriage—we both were very young, he was physically abusive, and we both had problems with drugs and alcohol. As a wife, lost in addiction at the time, I had been unfaithful to him. In the last days of my active use of chemicals, I had planned my suicide and wrote him a letter, confessing all that I had done, in hopes that he would forgive me for my part of what had happened in our marriage. Now, I was in recovery and had the need to make my amends.

I never gave him the letter, and as he sat wondering what this was all about, I sadly began the story of the broken young woman who had experienced tremendous pain in her life before we met, who should never have married him, and how much sorrow I had for what had gone on in our marriage. Tears streamed from my eyes. My heart had opened, and I sincerely felt the anguish.

He looked at me and said, "It's OK. Whenever anyone has said anything about you, I have always stood up for you."

Even as I write this, I did not fathom such unconditional love from this man. I looked at him and said, "Thank you. You no longer have to do that. I am now ready to take care of myself."

I felt as if I'd released him and myself from bondage that day. We both came to the realization that we should have never married. We were running from our family lives, and, in a sense, we were each other's saviors. I salvaged a friendship from the ruins, but he never made amends for his abusive treatment of me. Perhaps helping me when I needed help was his silent amends.

A Devoted Friendship

I had called my girlfriend's phone, and when I heard her say hello, I began to tell her of the difficulties I was experiencing in a relationship I was involved with. She tried to advise me to go on a different path than the one I was on.

Of course, I fought everything she suggested and decided to go my own way, in spite of what she had said. Right before we ended our call, she said, "I love you, and no matter what happens, I will always be here to help pick up the pieces again."

This woman was right and has remained my friend for thirty-six years now. She has picked up many pieces and has very special "Celeste glue."

A Young Man's Gift

I had decided to sell my house after twenty-three years of living with its wonderful care of me. I knew I needed help to accomplish this feat. I talked to friends about my plan, and some offered to help out in bits, but everyone worked and most had families. One day, a dear friend came to me and said, "Maybe my son will help you."

He brought his twenty-six-year-old son to my house one afternoon. I showed him around and told him what I needed. I said I would pay a fair wage for his help every day.

We stood in the kitchen as strangers, not really knowing each other except for an occasional hello when he was with his father.

He looked kindly at me and said, "I know you need the help, and I will be here for you whenever and however long it takes to complete this project." I knew he meant what he said.

We became great friends and spent hours, days, and months talking about life as he waded through my life with me, deciding what was either needed or no longer needed on this new journey. His gift to me was kindness and the generosity of his own heart. I honor him. He was a gift.

A Christmas Poinsettia

My youngest son came joyously in through the back door of the house, carrying the largest poinsettia I had ever seen, with a gigantic smile on his face. He set it in the middle of the dining room table, and it practically covered the whole table. He then turned and looked at me with a smile that lit up the room. "Merry Christmas, Mom. I love you!"

My heart melted as tears of joy filled my eyes.

Grandma's Love

My grandmother sat on her couch, watching her afternoon soap operas. I walked in and sat down next to her and lay my head on her lap. She looked sweetly down at me as she stroked my hair from my face and said, "Yeah, Grandma loves you." I just nestled into her lap and bathed in all that love. I knew she really did love me.

Words from My Hospital Social Worker

The lunch tray had just been collected, and I lay in my hospital bed, still 75 percent paralyzed from my near-death experience. One of my doctors had asked a hospital social worker to visit me. She arranged her chair right next to my bed so she could look at me when we talked. This woman was very kind and compassionate and came every day after lunch to talk with me. I admired the assertive strength she displayed as we spoke, and I believed in what she said to me.

Initially, it was small talk, as she got to know me a bit and found out I was a social worker myself, employed as a chemical-dependency counselor. Then one day, we chatted about my feelings.

"How do you feel about where you are in life?" she asked.

"I feel beaten down and somewhat hopeless right now," I said. "I have not yet been out of bed except by flat board. I am frail, and my energy is weak." I was teary-eyed as I said, "I don't know what will happen to me. I don't know if I will ever walk again, and I have no family that comes to visit me."

She was wonderfully empathic as she touched my arm and said, "I understand." She then looked me straight in the eye and said, "You need to take back the power in your life."

I was shocked. "How do I take back the power in my life when I cannot move my body, except for my head, forearms and hands?"

"Start by asking for what you need."

I thought this was a rather bold and profound statement, but after she left, I considered it and thought, *OK, I'll give it a go.*

My body was being turned every four hours, and it still experienced severe pain most of the time. All I thought about was my condition and how to get my body moving again. I thought about my son and his estrangement from me, and I cried—lots of crying because I was scared and alone.

When my nurse came in, I said, "I would like to be turned now."

"It's only been two hours since you were last turned," she said. "They'll be in to turn you in two more hours."

"But I would like to be turned now because I am in so much pain, lying in this position."

She looked surprised but smiled at me and then replied, "Let me see if I can find some help."

Soon, she returned with two others, and they turned me. I thanked them, and when they left, I thought of my social worker who had said, "You need to take back the power in your life." That day, I did!

Honest Words from My Mother

It was the spring of 2000, and I was about to depart for the university I was attending to present my clinical research paper to an audience of my peers. I stood in my living room, a few feet from my mother, and said, without any real intent behind my words, "You must be really proud of your children, both of us graduating college with our master's degrees."

She looked at me and said, "I am most proud of you. You are the one who had the hardest life."

Those were the only words that ever came from her heart to me.

Panic and Comfort

As I drove across a very long bridge on an interstate, I began to panic—I was lost. I was supposed to meet friends to go to a wedding, but I could not find them. Soon, I was overcome by a full-fledged panic attack. I'd never had one but had heard clients speak of them. I talked to myself to keep my focus as I drove across the bridge, looking for an exit ramp. One ahead—great! I turned the car toward it, and at the bottom of the ramp, I had to choose which direction to turn.

As I decided to turn right, I saw my friend's van go through the intersection, and I sped up to follow him and get his attention. When he finally saw me, he stopped, jumped out of his van, and came to my car. I hugged him and told him what had happened. With tears of joy, I said, "You were right where I needed you to be at the time when I needed you to be here."

The Power of Love and Healers

In my intuition class one evening, I told the story of the person I love who'd had a hemorrhagic stroke. Earlier that day, I had asked for healers and prayer warriors to share their healing gifts with him remotely. Approximately ninety beautiful people responded to my request, in this country and across the seas. I was overwhelmed by the love.

My teacher looked very thoughtfully and lovingly into my eyes and said, "God loves Trey as much as you love him. Now just sit back, and let God take care of him."

After class, so many offered hugs and prayers that I was spiritually overwhelmed.

The Wind Dancing

I have seen the wind dancing,
I've seen the calm rage,
I've felt the teardrops sting and the breath fade.
But never has my soul died.

Being Vulnerable

He brought me close, looked deeply into my soul through my mind's eye, and said, "I see you." I knew he had, and it was love that spoke.

International Conference

I walked into the room as it began to fill with faces, most of which I did not know. I was feeling anxious; I was about to present an experiential workshop I had written titled "Tune In, Turn On, Tune Up: Women, Empowerment, and Spirituality." I had never presented this workshop to anyone but always hoped one day it would become a reality. Now, there I was, the first time presenting it. Healing Beyond Borders had selected me to present at their international conference in Minneapolis, Minnesota. As I started to speak, I knew that I knew the material I was about to present. My voice needed to be strong, and my heart had to feel my message.

At the beginning of my presentation, I announced, "The topics we discuss today may cause feelings to arise that could be unsettling for you. If that should happen, I encourage you to seek professional counseling to guide you in working through these areas."

When exploring oneself, it is not unusual to have buried feelings surface.

One of the subtopics of the presentation was identifying messages learned as a child and how they are carried into adulthood. The attendees resonated with this topic.

I asked, "Has anyone learned an unspoken message that you continue to carry with you today?"

A woman said, "I learned as a child that if I did what others wanted, I would be accepted."

"Excellent example," I said.

Then she sadly announced, "I still find myself doing almost everything people ask me to do. I've never really looked at this before."

She saw herself as a people-pleaser. We discussed having our own voices and the ability to say no.

Another woman talked about her childhood. "I never felt safe being who I am. I tried to make myself invisible by staying out of everyone's way."

"How did it feel to spend your life hiding?" I asked.

She had tears in her eyes. "That is how I still am in my marriage. I have never been happy."

We discussed the thoughts, feelings, and behaviors that were carried forward, and we shared ideas about becoming authentic and speaking your truth and shedding the old messages and the falsehoods they carried.

One of the women in the class was a friend of mine; I had known her for twenty-five years. I learned of fears she had carried all of her life—she had never talked to me about them until that day in the workshop.

Two and a half hours later, after active participation—I'd worn a microphone for recording the presentation, and pictures were taken of the session—it was now over. I then invited the participants to go about their day in love and light. Many thanked me for helping them to see more of who they were; they thanked me for allowing their fears to surface and be known, and they thanked me for sharing my truth with them.

There was only one man in the workshop and after class, he disclosed, "Men experience the same fears and shame that women do, and I certainly have mine."

"Yes, they do," I agreed, "although men are taught different value systems that have denied them of sharing their feelings like women do." I thanked him for his bravery in sharing what he did in a class of all women.

Helping Hands, Loving Hearts

It was the summer of 1991. I'd just arrived home after being away for four months—I'd had a two-month hospital stay and another two months at the home of my boyfriend's parents after my near-death experience. I walked through the door of our rented duplex, and all of my eighteen-year-old son's furniture and dirty, moldy dishes were piled in the middle of the living room floor. I was in disbelief that he and my mother had just dumped his belongings there and left this for me to take care of, when I had just come through a near-death experience, been totally paralyzed, and was alone. I barely had time to catch my breath from the sight when there was a knock at the door.

There they all were, the close friends I had made in a city where I'd lived for not yet a year, with smiles on their faces and hugs abundant. They looked around, said very little about what they saw, and told me they were there to clean the house. They invited me to lie down and rest. A couple of hours later, we were all sitting around, laughing and telling stories. Friendship and overwhelming love beyond words entered my door that day.

Foster Care Savior

My last year of high school was soon to start, and my mother had decided it was time again to send me somewhere to live, other than with her. She did this quite often; I had been to many schools for short periods. I never really had the chance to make friends or build any kind of relationship with anyone. She and I had never bonded as mother and daughter, for obvious reasons. Now, she had contacted the court system and said that she could not handle me, that I was out of control; she requested that I be placed in foster care.

The environment I had grown up in, with abusive alcoholism and narcissism, provided very little direction. If you did not serve a purpose in my mother's life, you were easily discarded. I never was in any trouble. I was not on probation or under the court's jurisdiction. I lived a life of values that I had set for myself and adhered to this standard as much as a child from a broken, abusive, alcoholic home could do.

On this particular day, I had to appear in front of the judge for determination as to whether I would be placed in foster care. He escorted me into his chamber, and as we talked, he said, "I'm sorry, Celeste. Unfortunately, we cannot take the parent out of the home."

We returned to the courtroom, where my mother sat, and I felt defeated, with nothing more I could do. What had I done besides live in hell during my life? Yet now, I faced going somewhere else she wanted to send me.

I heard the heavy wooden courtroom door open, and we turned our heads to see who was approaching. A voice from behind me said, "Your Honor, I would like to take Celeste home to live with me." It was my brother.

The judge granted the request, and I lived with my brother during my senior year of high school, which was the best year of my young life. He has always been my hero for stepping in and being a parent to me at such a young age.

The Eraser

Each step I take comes with a decision.
My mind has much chatter, each with its own expectation.
Where does this come from?

I unroll the scroll that has lived well inside, each line from someone or perhaps an experience that comes to life, as if it is jumping from the very paper it is written on. A brief or sometimes lengthy review brings a conclusion. I try it on for size. Hmmm.

Seems to fit, but is it fruitful? Another choice.

By the time I take the next step, the process begins once more.
After time is seen to be dwindling, I stop for a moment, look around, I see an eraser.

I once again, look at the scroll, a tear, a smile, a sigh of relief, rub, rub, rub.

The door opens to my heart, and the light shines, beautifully brilliant, I kiss the morning and feel at peace.

Removing a layer of costume,
Exposing yet another view of me,
Slowly unfolding, another Light shines,
I know you are seeing me as I am each time,
More wonderment, more wondering, more wonderful!

Such Sweet Nectar

Day was ending. I was about to turn off the lights when a text message came through my cell phone. I opened it, and the message read, "Good night, beautiful angel."

Spirit Light—My Love from Previous Lives Ago

It was a warm fall evening in 2018. My girlfriend Julie and I went to a venue where a dear friend of mine was performing. He orchestrated and was the front man of a famous Prince tribute band. His build was lean, and he had black collar-length hair. He dressed in black mirrored pants and a black velvet shirt with a purple floral design. He also wore black higher-heeled boots. He danced a bit on stage and performed mini skits to select songs he would sing with a female member of the band, who danced at times during the performance. He was quite dashing in appearance, with a voice that was soft-spoken—until he began to sing. Spiritually, he was very connected to Prince, and his performances were channeled often by Prince's energy when he was on stage.

When the show was over and the music ended, he retreated to his dressing room until most of the fans had left for the night. Because of his celebrity status and his handsome, charismatic character, people loved being near him. Most of the time, when there were many people present to see him, he made his way through the crowds with bodyguards at his sides. His close friends were also quite protective of him.

About a half an hour later, only two fans remained by the dressing room door, so he stepped out and spoke with them. He was aware of my presence at a table not far from where he stood. Slowly, he started moving backward from the fans, thanking them for coming to his performance that evening. As he came closer, I extended my arm out from my side, and he softly moved into it, as if he knew it was waiting for him. As my hand gently touched the lower part of his back, he turned into me and put his arms around me and held me.

He then put his hands on my upper arms, held me away from him, and said, with a sweet and loving smile on his face, "You are so beautiful."

He then put his arms around me again, with our hearts touching, as he kept whispering, "I love you, I love you, I love you," over and over again. After some time, he stepped back and looked in my eyes and said, "There you are! You have dimples! There you are! Can you see me?"

I could see him, but what we saw was from a life many lifetimes ago. Oh, how I love him. Words do not express my feelings for him. There are no words, only vibrations, frequencies, *love*. I said softly, "I love you."

He pulled me close to him again, and this time, as our hearts danced together, he whispered in my ear, "Does this resonate with you?" and he began to hum.

"Yes," I said and relaxed into the soothing tone of his voice.

"There you are," he said. I smiled from cheek to cheek. I knew he could see me, that he loved me, and that he would never leave me. He had told me some time ago that he never would. He then kissed me, but we realized there were many people around us and knew our time had to end.

As we said goodbye, we touched each other with outstretched hands. He smiled and said, "Send me a message when you get home so I know you arrived there safely."

I smiled warmly and said, "I will."

Then he called out, "I will see you," and I replied, "Soon!"

I turned and floated across the dance floor.

We knew each other, spiritually and energetically, from past lives. In our soul contract, we must have agreed to meet each other again this time around. It was such a delight to be together. Sometimes, we only spoke telepathically to each other, but he said we spoke volumes without verbal language, and I knew that well.

My Oldest Son's Father

Oh, how time rushes over us like a waterfall
Washing away, eroding, bringing new life

It was a cloudy afternoon, and I was gazing at books in my bookcase. I noticed my yearbooks from so long ago beckoning me to pick them up and look through them. I was feeling rather nostalgic, so I thought, *Why not?*

As I read through my tenth-grade yearbook—a time when I struggled greatly due to the constant, pending uncertainty of always being sent to live with someone else because my mother didn't have the skills to parent a child—I came across a page that was filled with writing toward the very end of the book. Gazing at the words on the page, I remembered and whispered, "Oh, how long ago this was, yet how fresh it still is in my mind."

The words written below were penned by my oldest son's father before he enlisted in the armed services. As I read the words, my heart longed for that feeling once again, the innocence of a time that was, and the innocence of a childhood that lay dormant for decades that followed:

Dearest Celeste,

I want to wish you all the luck in the world for the coming years in the future that you have ahead of you. We've only known each other for about eight months, but we've gotten to know each other pretty well in that time.

I hope you'll always remember all the things I've ever told you. If you do, things will always work out for the better. Try to be a good girl, and try to make the best out of everything. Stay with the right people, and be the way I'd want you to. Do real good in your next two years of school. They'll count the most. Get into some other activities in school. Do the best in everything you do. Remember all the good times we've had together. I'll never forget all the things we did. I'll never forget you either. Though we may not see each other for a very long time, I'll always remember you as the really sweet person that you are. Let the outside appearance show what you are really like on the inside. Remember, The <u>Good Guys</u> are the <u>Best</u>. Be the <u>best</u>. Do it just for me.

Til I see you again,

Love you Much,

P.S. <u>Always look ahead.</u>

I was fifteen years old at the time of this writing. As I look back at this, my heart still weeps. He was the father of my first son, and he didn't even know it until some years later.

I'm including a valentine from this man of so many decades ago, sent to me for Valentine's Day 2019. For many years, he remembered me on this occasion, Mother's Day, and Christmas.

A Valentine [from my oldest son's father]

Over the years of our life, through joys and strife, one thing remained the same, like knowing your name.

We had great times a long time ago, and which caused us to remain friends always this we know. We have a bond that never will be broken; it is real inside us, not just a token.

Through distance and time we always remain; something inside is always the same.

You meant a lot to me and found a place in my heart, like great memories we shall never part.

So I wish you many happy thoughts of things in your life, that we shared through any strife.

Some bonds are broken but ours shall never die; we share something that created a tie.

So have a happy V Day and put on the smiles, because I am thinking of you over all the many miles.

So be my Valentine again as we always do, as we share those memories that keep coming through. Happy Valentine's Day. I love having you in my life.

Your forever lover

The reason I've included these heartfelt messages is to acknowledge this relationship in honor of my first son and the love I have for him.

My Heart, Your Space

As my soul takes flight,
When my body takes its final rest for the day,
And has found its slumber,
May you remember the space I hold for you,
As the angels smile, standing quietly by your side.

11

Lifting the Veil

The Nightshade so proudly displayed in the
Garden of Blarney Castle now lifts its iron dome
And becomes beauty so long hidden
from secrets long ago

Looking back over my life, it's as if I viewed the journey through a looking glass. I write about this in a rather deep sense that magnifies the intensity of feelings that surround or shroud the image of who I was. At times, I have glimpses of the wounded child who carries her armor, just in case, as she still finds her guard.

What follows depicts my feelings and what I have seen through my spiritual third eye. This is what resonates within my soul as I see the past with my psychic gifts—what the souls of many have experienced.

As I walked through the corridor of voices, sometimes silent, sometimes heard, this traveler found her eyes and ears, which made sense of the chatter—the tongues of many long ago and less so in the present. At times, the cries were excruciating, soul-felt; at other times, soothing. Most of the time, however, they were critical and demeaning. Each wall along the tunnel of growth had its own face. I recognized them all. Each step forward brought another voice, another face. Why was such pain and anguish always present and always on this journey? The pain from generations past—my heart wept for them all.

As a child, I saw the faces and heard the voices and held them within. No one to talk to; no one who understood. I felt different than anyone else. I heard the music in the trees and their soft whispers and felt safe. Above all, I lingered, knowing that once I took the step downward, I would enter into their world again—the anger, the cruelty, the tears. Could they not recognize their own pain, or was it easier to continue to hide?

I am the product of what was planted. The seed began to grow, and finally, at gestation, my bud opened and blossomed into a beautiful little plant that needed to be watered and spoke gently to. Instead, she was showcased in her lovely Christmas dress—white bodice, with the skirt decorated in bright-red velvet poinsettias and a red velvet ribbon that adorned the waist. Oh, how lovely she was, with her long golden hair, as she knelt in front of the Christmas tree. A camera flashed, and the Polaroid ejected a picture of this fair child. Her white anklets with lace around the top edge and black patent leather shoes made it the perfect Christmas picture. The voices and faces barked orders on how to sit, not to talk, smile, be still, hauntingly hover over the photo today.

As the walk through time became more labored, I realized the corridor was elevating slightly, and the faces on the walls were changing. Barking orders, then silent, then screaming, then sobbing. These were the faces of those who became the dictators of this ever-changing journey.

At times, I walked evenly; at other times, the terrain was quite rocky. Faces from every direction demanded more, always more. Why couldn't they see I was giving my best? Why was it never good enough? The tears that filled my eyes became more frequent, and sadness lay heavily upon my heart, like an anvil, with a never-ending pounding that slowly was breaking me.

So much loss, so much sickness in my life—would it never end? An ocean of tears and a heart now beating erratically. The faces and voices slightly changed, and it was now whether I would live or leave. My soul, though fractured, and my heart, broken, would not give up; it had been blessed with compassion and a strength to not only survive but to live. Although many times my body was knocked down into a dark pit, it always found a way out; at times, there were steps, and at other times, I crawled, but I always came out.

One particular day, the corridor came to a T, and I had to make a decision on which pathway to travel. I heard a voice that I had not heard since I was a child: "You never know when the miracle will happen." I knew then that I must pick up the shadow of myself and move forward. My health came back. My angel appeared in the form of a five-foot-three

Filipino man, who inspired me to "Don't stop believin'." I recovered from my illness, and the diseases were being healed. I knew it was time to make decisions, and I did.

Although I had not traveled this path before, it was the one I was to take. I had much confusion about religion while growing up. On Sunday, I was to go to Sunday school, but Saturday night was reserved for witnessing brutal beatings. "Good morning, Sunday school teachers and other children I don't know"; nor did they know me. We would have a story about Jesus, who was God's son, and then eat a cookie and drink Kool-Aid. Dismissed. From that point on, it was being in temples and singing and chanting in the desert, to something that seemed to bring peace into my existence, if only briefly.

Years of longing, wondering—*What is all this about?*—finally directed me to answers that led me within. There was dissection of my inner being, more tears, more questions, and a turning point—the demise of the loudest and most condemning voice. As I sat at the death bed and heard the moans and groans of life's agony, the tortured face of a lifetime of anger now was silenced. There was an eruption of unconditional love from my heart as I consoled the victim who had caused so much anguish and turmoil for me and for others, who now lay there, writhing in pain, as I used divine-source energy to soothe the suffering as the soul left the body.

In order to rid myself of toxicity and negativity, I used a technique that requests archangel Michael to remove energetic cords that run between souls, to be cut. By calling in this archangel and asking for his spiritual assistance, I experienced the freedom of cord-cutting in spirit, to now bask in my own divine energy, my own self.

My teachers came in swiftly, and the shift brought a lifetime before my eyes. As I elevated, more of me was revealed, until I came to the question, "What am I now ready to let go of?" As I sat in the silence of who I am, my senses were stimulated by the essential oil geranium, an oil that aids in "releasing." I asked Divine Source to guide me in releasing fear, unworthiness, inadequacy, being unlovable, low self-worth and low self-esteem, and the feelings of not being good enough.

After this cleansing, what was I left with? A clean slate that I could clear every evening and start over with each day. A feeling of worthiness, of being loved, of being enough. Was it easy? Nothing was easy in my world, but was it worthwhile? *Yes!*

Today, my smile shines from the inside out. Do I ever cry? Oh yes, sometimes often, but now I know why. Does the hurt ever show itself from days gone by? Absolutely. But I now know why I am crying, and I know how to stop the tears. The woundedness of my soul continues to need nurturing, but today, I can do that. No chemicals, food, or drink soothes me. I now soothe myself with the constant supply of loving guides, angels, and divine-source energy that lovingly nurtures me whenever I ask.

Is life perfect? I'm not sure I have the definition of what that means. I do know that there continue to be challenges. We live on earth school. I came here not only to herald in the New Age as a Pleiadian child but also to fulfill a soul contract I made before coming here—or, in lighter terms, was born. I have learned many lessons since I have been here again, and I know there is at least one that I still need to learn. It is taking a very long time for this lesson, but I also know that if I am to learn it, I must be patient. Time on earth is measured linearly, but time in spirit does not exist.

My lesson is still in spirit, developing as I continue to work on becoming a better version of my highest self. My lover is also learning in spirit, and when we both are ready, this incredible love story we have lived for the past several years in spirit will manifest in the physical. Then, learning to honor it and cherish it will continue until I exit this life on earth. I see the differences each day, and I am amazed!

We are all interconnected. We are all brothers and sisters in spirit, and we all have lessons to learn while we are here. Be mindful of what you bless others with, for it is the nectar that reveals who you are. When you leave, what will be your legacy?

An Excerpt from Life

I have seen the tears of countless souls as they've sat in my confidence—sad, heartbroken, afraid, terrified, beaten, and broken.

There have been countless stories of anger, sickness, disease, bitterness, lost love, destruction, suicide, and torture.

There were cuts on their arms, stomachs, upper thighs, and chests, where no one would see.

There were tattooed bodies and faces, done not for beauty or statement but to hide, like a mask, their pain.

I have heard the cries, the screams, the pleading, and bargaining of the torment deep within, and my heart has wept.

I've prayed, chanted, worked with energy, listened to stories of the heartbroken and battered, cried with them, and cried alone, always wondering why. Why is the soul a container for such loss that eternally embeds the tragedies of time?

Perhaps there, in the shadows, may be found that flicker of contentment or joy that passes through, bringing an excitement of hope, that one day it will be different.

Every loss, every pain, every sickness serves as its own vehicle. It is only at the crossroad that we stop for a moment and see—truly see—who we are, who we have become, and who we wish we were. If the pain is too great, we succumb to it, but how many find their strength in that moment to choose to turn?

Who am I? I am one who chose to turn. Yes, I have my own container and continue to sort through it and make peace and release. It is in recognition and forgiveness of the past that I have found the underlying peace, allowing love to find its own avenue.

My light and love are who I am—the flickering light of God, a beacon, always showing me, *hope.*

Peace and love be to all who read these pages and that you will come to know *you* through the eyes of love.

The Frequency

All love surrounds us like raindrops from the sea
Light crystal memories bring happiness to me
Bright sparkling dew from the trees whisper that we
Sing now a new song that we are free

Give me an angel to watch over me
Bring me the moonlight that I might be
Colors from heaven the ecstasy
Keeps me in tune with the frequency

12

The Light of Awareness

As a child, we do not walk in the ways of the world,
but rather dodge the bullets of what comes and
hope we make it through yet in this life.

As I wrote each brief memory, I relived the past and very well could have viewed what I wrote as a tragedy of lost youth, lost relationships, lost love. Instead, I chose to read it as a love story, a breakthrough from the bondage of the past into the new awakening of the present and, more importantly, the reckoning and the atonement of what was to what is.

With the recognition of the fractured heart of my soul, which has searched for eternity to heal, it is in this lifetime that I am coming together with my soul pod, my soul family. I have met again my husband from lifetimes past, who was also my father and my canine in different lifetimes, who loves me dearly in this life. My dear spiritual friend who reads tarot cards told me that he came back for me. When I thanked him for doing so, he said, "Even knowing the vast difficulties I would face in the first chapters of this life, the choice to return was quite easy to make." The first time we saw each other, we knew, without a doubt, that we had been together before.

I continue to hold space for the most incredible love in my life. (I wrote about him earlier as my "current love.") I have been with him for numerous lifetimes. Spirit tells me that we are together now just because we love each other. It has been a choppy road for us because my ascension has happened throughout this lifetime, but as time proceeds, his ascension is quickening. Many physical challenges have occurred, including his tragic stroke, but our love for each other continues to bless our pathway.

The struggle in this life is not in living but in living life to your fullest potential, without the interference of ego or of self-defeating messages that have an endless tape running in constant motion, without regard for admonishment.

In my career as a psychotherapist, which has continued for decades, my biggest awareness has been that I have seen the challenge against self—some generational, some this lifetime. Regardless of the time frame, it remains a debacle.

Years of programming, prebirth through death, have wound toxicity into every crevice, slowly eating away, willfully, wantonly, without regard for the inner self—the self that cries and sits in the therapist's office, with tears streaming down their cheeks; the tears of a man in his late-senior years because his father never asked if he was okay after saving his sister's life, when he was seven years old and she was five, after a stampede of horses ran through the yard where they were playing.

Or the ninety-plus-year-old beautiful woman who softly wept as she sat across from me because her husband no longer saw her as being sexually attractive and ignored her modest intentions of affection.

Becoming aware of self is not a project that one does in the way one studies for a test; rather, it's a lifelong conscious awakening—and then another lifelong conscious awakening. We have much to learn, and in each incarnation, there are more lessons to learn.

As you become more aware of your surroundings, your behaviors, and your actions, you also attune to your feelings.

Many have been "trained" on someone else's idea of what it is to be you. A word of enlightenment here: *no one knows what it is like to be you*. No one knows what you know; no one sees what you see, hears what you hear, feels the way you do—no one. At best, we can only attempt to relate to a circumstance that is similar to one we have ourselves experienced.

Our entire time on earth school is a learning venture. We have a constant barrage of orders, suggestions, fears, secrets, jealousies, competition, anger (passed on in the name of "for your own good" or my own, or someone's expectation or disappointment), which leaves us living in a puzzle that doesn't quite seem to have all the pieces when we try to put it together. We wander around—at times, aimlessly—because none of it makes sense, but if this is what I am told, then I had better do it. No one ever wants to be left out or left behind, so you slowly comply with what you are told; perhaps happiness or joy eludes you but only because you have not found the correct puzzle pieces yet.

The next time you hear yourself telling someone they "should"—*stop!* You have no idea what "should" be; you can only share your experience and quietly allow others to decide if what you have said fits for them. *One size does not fit all!* Simply allow all the experience that is meant to be, unless you are aware of imminent danger of some sort, so the lesson to be learned will be presented.

Do not live simply to put in your time. We are not punching a time clock, although it may seem like it; rather, it's a spot of linear time, mapped out and decided upon before birth. This is your time, whether long or short; you are here for the reasons you chose before you came here, before your incarnation.

As the sun shines, so does the soul. Many will experience a dark night of the soul, and it often manifests as a spiritual crisis. Time length varies. I have experienced more than one shadow period, and the first occurred when I had my near-death experience. The second occurred after my year of significant losses. Both were incredible turning points in my life that led to a greater spiritual awakening.

This is not to be feared; it's more a time of mirroring, a deep reflection of soul-searching. This may feel uncomfortable and, at times, may even be a painful chapter in life. Nonetheless, view the experience as an important period of growth.

If you find this happening, be cognizant of the lessons presented to you; all are for learning and growing the aspects of the spiritual self. The ascension into awareness of a higher dimension will readjust your inner compass, and you will see life with renewed vision.

As our frequencies heighten, we experience feelings of lightness, as if walking on a translucent cloud, the energy of which swirls around and through us, with a slight shift in how we view ourselves and the world around us. As I shift, quite often I become softer, easier, calmer; situations that used to be filled with drama are not as important. I used to do things for my family out of fear of being rejected. I used to have the need to fit in so I would feel accepted. I used to stay drugged or drunk so I could handle reality.

I now know how easy it was to be caught in others' energy fields and how to protect myself from this, although, at times, it still happens. It is more like, at first recognition, I am able to place a protective shield around my aura, my etheric body, and I then find myself viewing the circumstance, more as a movie. I learn from the movie; I am not part of the acting out of the movie. Such a wonderful relief, getting to know others through these eyes

We do have a choice of what we want to do with our lives. The incredible ability we have to change our paths from victim to being the captain of the ship lies within our being.

We are such unique individuals, traveling this path, this journey, and how we choose to view our time here is our choice. Sometimes, physical limitations present challenges for the physical body, or disturbances in cognition will not allow cognitive understanding. What I am speaking of, however, is the spiritual being that experiences this space-time continuum.

The beautiful light beings that sparkle and twinkle bring beauty to our souls. We are magnets of wonderfulness. Once you recognize this within yourself, others already will have recognized it. The contrast is amazing!

Coming Home

Only when the softest petal gently lands upon the earth,
Only when you feel the whisper of a breeze,
Only when your heart is freely opened will you know,
I have been the Shadow of a thousand lifetimes,
Coming home to you.

13

The New Age

As the Shade lifts, so shall my Eye open.

I would like to reflect on areas of my life that I found significant on my spiritual journey. The years of trauma, enlightenment, and sickness have broadened the scope of how I view life. Each area I have written about thus far has allowed a glimpse into tragedy and love—how the unlearning of trauma unfolded in my subconscious mind, through neuroplasticity, to create change in my brain, through new thought processes and coping skills.

I taught my clients to change behaviors, as I had pioneered the pathway for this teaching method by healing myself first. When I introduced them to the therapeutic relationship, I encouraged them by saying, "I will never ask you to do something that I have not previously done for myself."

Now, to take a deeper dive into what I have learned, I will address how I see life. Some of what I've learned I credit to outside sources. The inner knowing extends from my psychic gifts and what I have seen in spirit.

As we each enter this spectacular New Age, it is necessary for me to add a few words regarding space-time inclusions. The marriage of science and metaphysical theorems allow for humans to function in the space-time continuum, as well as experience the timeless constraint of spirit. For over four billion years, humans have inhabited this planet called earth on a continuous learning cycle.

We have traveled through many ages, as science reveals with extensive documented studies. The expansion, at least in the Western world, since its inclusion of metaphysical (beyond physical) theoretical studies, proves the existence of a completely different paradigm of thought, which shifts to a continuum of life after death of the physical body (Jesús Silva

Bautista, Venazir Herrera Escobar, Rodolfo Corona Miranda, "Psychological Study on the Origin of Life, Death and Life after Death: Differences between Beliefs According to Age and Schooling," *Universal Journal of Educational Research* 6, no. 6 (2018): 1175–1186, http://www.hrpub.org DOI: 10.13189/ujer.2018.060607).

We shed the suit or costume we perceptually developed while in the physical realm and release the soul, the aliveness of who we truly are, into the timeless void. We exist as a vapor of consciousness, transitioning in an energetic form that science recognizes as quantum physics or the expansive, infinite matrix of energy, which may be manipulated by both man and spirit. I explain, in an effort for understanding, that which connects us, as humans, to the spirit world in the journey of the healing of my fractured soul.

There is so much to explore, and we, as humans, are quite limited, if we only view what *is* as science. Expanding your stillness by meditation allows for a melding of body and soul to recognize the vastness that awaits; that thought is often limited, and spirit is limitless.

As I journeyed through the toxicity and generational conditioning, which was passed on as the model of my perceived spectrum, as a child into young adulthood, I became ever more conscious of the world around me and the world within me. Through extensive education and a mind that challenges the existence of who I am and who you are, I am each day absorbing the spiritual realm and remaining mindful, which means living in this moment and in each moment. I become present in the reality I am creating, one that is inclusive of all that I learn and all that I unlearn, as I move forward.

Each day becomes more delightful, as fear and uncertainty shed their age-old chains and create a clarity of aliveness, which I believe Divine Source has orchestrated wonderfully and has provided for all.

Being able to look within has changed my perception of without. My small space expands with each new experience, a gift given because I opened myself to receiving.

So you see, a remarkable balance has been revealed in this writing. Life, the magical roller coaster that is never ending, has provided equal amounts of loss and gain, not to be perpetuated but rather mixed up, by allowing each of us to become the artist, owning a rich palette of color to paint what we choose. But in doing so, we must surrender to the unlearning and trust the process of life. No matter what the context, we are still the artist, and spirit remains within to offer color.

The Story

Down the cobblestone once cluttered,

Lies an untold story, one of mystery, one of intrigue,

Each must consider the road to travel,

For to start and quit is loss indeed.

> I have come to believe that my mind thinks in iambic
> pentameter. It breathes a flow, the music of my soul.

The list of stories is endless—of lost love, lost life, lost love. Always lost love. We are searching constantly for the other. Some search shamelessly for a lifetime, and they continue to miss each other. "Why?" we may ask. I do not have the answer to the mystery of love, but I do know, from what I have lived, that the woundedness of the soul—or perhaps even the woundedness of the ego—keeps those apart who are meant to be together. I've read many accounts of those who were meant to be but let love slip away, sometimes out of fear; sometimes heartbreak from the one from whom a lesson was meant only to be learned.

It is in the evenings, when darkness falls upon the earth and shadows become heightened, that we face the truth—our own truth. Loneliness is, has been, and always will be, unless we heal our fractured hearts, our fractured souls, and allow the light, the love to come in. Be vulnerable again where fear reigns; take the risk, toss away the wind that blows out the lamp of reason, and walk in dignity, shamelessly, forward on our path, for it is ours alone that leads to the other.

I *am*, I am, I *am*, I *am* truth, light, love. The flame of a thousand candles, the song of endless lifetimes, and the divine source that lives within all. The separation, the duality, comes only in thought, not in frequency.

We are each a connected energy with the other. We vibrate at our own frequencies through a vast network of energy, wanting to be a note in the song. The crown of creation is all around us. Will you shine your stone in that crown? Will you sing me the song my heart longs to hear, only from your notes, when singled out, and soothingly, will we become our own song? Together, can you hear it? Throw away the shroud that covers your nakedness and stand at the top of the hill, claim it, and care for it. It is waiting. I am waiting. I am waiting. I *am* waiting.

The cries from the halls of addiction, the cries from the halls of the inner mind. Look into my eyes; what do you see? What do you really see? Do you see me or a reflection of you? We are all one, and we are all the same. Only the costumes are different, making it easy to label. Again, if I stood before you naked, in all of my truth, would I be safe? Can you say yes and make it your truth?

As the windows of the soul are washed with the tears of yesterday, cleansing happens, and we begin to see. Please see me. I am the child of the past, the mother, the wife, the worker, the teacher, the caregiver, the seamstress, the lover, the lonely, the abused, the discounted, the threatened, the lost.

Whispering Winds

As the whisper of winds playfully tease the crisp leaves still remaining,
I hear the laughter of endless lifetimes generating energy.
The wisdom of the trees, sharing knowledge of ancient time,
Humming a rhythmic song so familiar that the frequency finds me,
I smile, knowing that I too have danced that tune,
The arms of life surround me as the envelope seals and I *am*
Everlasting Light.

14

And So It Is

Oh Divine Source,

Bring us gently into the Light of who we are,

That we are one.

How blessed I have been to come into being who I am. I continue working with my amazingly wise spiritual teachers, learning about releasing and allowing my beautiful connection with spirit. The prophetic gifts with which I am now in tune continue developing, and I believe this will be lifelong, as more is revealed. Releasing so much of what was and allowing in the new continuum is sometimes a journey I must take with just myself or my spiritual teachers, but I joyfully learn from all.

My intuition is teaching me more each day, as I learn to rely on it for guidance instead of my ego, which, at times, has me reacting instead of feeling my way with my heart. My intuition is my friend, and it is my lifeline to God, to spirit, to Divine Source. Blending spirit and body allows for a smoother transport in the complicated world we call home for just a short while. When our bodies return to dust and our souls once again occupy the vastness of heaven or the great I AM, we will all be united once more, until the restlessness of experience again yearns to explore. For we are the music; we are the song. Row your boat, gently down the stream, for life merely is but a dream. Life merely *is* but a dream.

And as she stood tall at the top of the mountain,

Her veil gently shifted with the breeze.

I heard the echoes of a thousand voices,

The angels applauding.

No longer hidden,

The veil fell to the ground, floating away like a cloud.

And her nakedness was her beauty,

Her Light shined,

All was in harmony with Divine love,

And her Truth released her,

Her Truth set her Free.

Afterword

As I neared the completion of this memoir, I was diagnosed with a growth in my bladder.

A cystoscopy was performed at Mayo Clinic. As the camera traveled up into my bladder, both the doctor doing the exam and I saw this growth swaying about inside of me.

He said, "Well, that shouldn't be there."

"No, it shouldn't!" I said.

What I saw was a growth shaped like a broccoli floweret. It was pinkish-red, and as I viewed down onto the top of it, I saw rings, like on the inside of a tree that tells its age. The rings were wavy and almost a lime green in color. At the bottom of its stem and around it on the wall of my bladder was a dark-red color. The doctor said that was "carpeting." I was amazed at what was growing inside of me. My mind was stunned and really had no comprehension of what this meant. It was as if I was viewing a movie. I guess, in a sense, I was, and I was the main character.

After this astonishment, I visited with a urologist, who seemed quite a compassionate specialist. She spoke gently yet directly to me and explained, "There are different stages of cancer, and after the surgeon removes the tumor, it will be sent to the lab for examination. Once it is determined if the cancer is in early, middle, or late stages, we will discuss what form of action to take. If it is in the early stage, as I suspect it is, due to the size of the tumor and no other visible tumors indicated, it will be removed, and chemotherapy administered at the time."

I did all I could to hold back the tears, as I felt them welling up in my eyes and throat. I could feel the fear racing through my body, but I could not cry. For some unknown reason, I was unable to allow my feelings to be known. I felt numb and in a trancelike state and just sat there. After the word *cancer* echoed from my doctor's voice, my hearing seemed to shut down.

I now know the importance of being accompanied by another to a visit that is potentially life-changing. I walked out of the doctor's office with bits and pieces of words echoing in the chambers of my mind and an impending doom surrounded me. *Cancer.* Everyone dreads the word, and, of course, my mind was focused on the horror stories that are shared. I found myself talking to God in my head—or rather, pleading, "Please, dear God. Don't let the tumor be cancerous."

When I finally left the clinic and started my hour-and-a-half journey home again, I was numb. I felt like I had just visited an alternate reality, and it was surreal.

While driving, my car phone notified me of an incoming call. A dear friend of mine, who had experienced bladder cancer herself, was calling to find out what the test results had revealed. As I shared my account of the appointment I had just completed, I began to cry.

Her soothing voice was so nurturing and loving. "I know this is hard for you. I remember how I felt when I was told I had bladder cancer. My doctor was kind and gentle and helped me to understand what he was telling me. It sounds like the cancer is in the early stages, and that is very good. You may only have to continue with follow-up visits to make sure it doesn't reappear." She knew exactly what I needed to hear at that moment. During our conversation, she asked, "Do you mind if I notify our Healing Touch group and ask them to send light and remote healing for you?"

I was filled with gratitude by the kindness of her gesture. "Please do," I said. "I would so appreciate their healing."

When I arrived home, I sent a message to the beautiful prayer warriors who have seen me through so much, asking once again for prayer. I also contacted the healers I knew for remote healing. So many responded to my requests, and I could feel my consciousness rising into a blissful state that calmed my being.

By dinnertime that evening, I was extremely elevated and visualized having a lilac growing inside of me. My interpretation of the lilac was a beautifully scented flower that bloomed, withered, and blew away. So much incredible healing energy filled me and remained. I was lovingly emptied of sadness and fear.

Surgery was scheduled for five days later because the blood thinners I was prescribed for atrial fibrillation in my heart had to be cleared from my body before surgery; if not, it could result in dire consequences. So for five days, I had to make a decision: I could feel sorry for myself and be miserable, or I could live for the day and be grateful. I chose living for the day and being grateful for it!

The morning of surgery arrived at an accelerated rate. My wonderful longtime friend accompanied me on my unknown journey. I reluctantly left her in the clinic waiting area and followed the nurse to the prep room to be prepared for surgery.

After she placed the IV in my arm and I answered a scroll of questions, my anesthesiologist popped in to visit. His daughter lived a block from me, and we chatted about the lovely area where I lived.

He then asked, "How are you feeling?"

"Naturally, somewhat anxious."

He smiled. "I have something for you that will take that feeling away."

I happily agreed. Before I was taken to surgery, his "something" had calmed me, and I was ready to go.

In the operating room, the angels were with me—archangel Michael and archangel Raphael, my grandmother's spirit, my father's spirit, and my sweetheart's spirit. I said, "OK, my beautiful Lord, everyone is present. Let's get this done!"

The doctor peered down at me. He placed a mask over my nose and mouth and told me to breathe deeply. He then said, "Nighty-night. I will see you later."

The next thing I knew, with my eyes still closed, I thought, *Yes, I can move my hands.* I moved them both, and I heard the nurse say, "How are you, Celeste?" I slowly opened my eyes, and there was my nurse, smiling at me and asking how I felt. Surgery is such an intriguing experience. Usually, when I come out, I am in pain, and it is quite a feat to get back to "the new normal." Not that day, though.

I felt happy that it was over. I then asked if it was cancer.

She said, "Yes, but the doctor said it was only about a centimeter in size, and he took it all. No signs of any more."

I was so thrilled!

The catheter was removed from my bladder, and I was administered chemotherapy. The chemotherapy was held inside of me for an hour; then flushed out with water. My friend was there, doing Healing Touch on me during this time, and I basked in gratitude.

I thanked God, the angels, and all of my loved ones for bringing me through surgery safely and now being cancer-free. I will have quarterly checkups for a while and then less frequently, to ensure it hasn't reappeared.

I returned home for one week, tired and healing, and became very ill. I had all the symptoms that would indicate the flu. There was something invading my body that had not been problematic after my surgery. I kept getting sicker as the days continued. This sickness had nothing to do with my surgery or the chemotherapy that had been administered. Friends encouraged me to go to Urgent Care or the emergency room, but I was too weak to even go to the kitchen to try to eat.

I finally called a dear friend and asked if she could take me to Urgent Care, and she drove right over. She took my arm as she helped me to the car, but before I walked out the door, my intuition adamantly stated, "Take your cell phone cord along." I thought it odd, but I put it in my purse. I have learned to listen to my intuition.

Two hours later and after several tests were completed, I was on my way to the hospital. *Always listen to your intuition!* I arrived around 8:15 p.m. and was immediately treated as if I had COVID-19. All staff were gowned and gloved and were wearing COVID-19 face gear that seemed to be a take-off of Darth Vader's helmet.

They spoke through a microphone-type apparatus that was on the COVID-19 mask. In the ER suite, a negative ionizer was operating, and precautions were high. I had my second COVID-19 test in two weeks at that time.

I had six hours of testing between my heart and abdomen. Due to experiencing heaviness in my chest, a heart problem had to be ruled out. As I was about to be placed in the CT scan tube, there was a call from my ER doctor, asking the technicians to include scans of my abdomen. Initially, the CT scan was only to check my lungs to rule out a pulmonary embolism, as I had experienced one in previous years.

After the tests were reviewed, a second doctor visited me. He said, "You do not have COVID. I know COVID, and you do not have it."

I was relieved. Shortly after his visit, my primary ER doctor reported, "You have diverticulitis. I'll be admitting you."

At 3:30 a.m., I was in my new hospital room. *Again*, when intuition says to take your phone cord, be sure to do so. I had nothing else, but I did have my phone cord!

Three days later, a taxi delivered me home, and I began my recovery from not only bladder cancer surgery but also diverticulitis.

At this writing, I am finally getting my strength back. Two days in a row, I went out for short walks, and it was wonderful to be out among the trees and flowers again. I love taking pictures of nature; secretly, nature loves to smile for the camera!

One of my editors asked me if I thought the "dark ball of energy" was present in my body again. No, I do not believe so. The area affected was my first and second chakras—my root chakra and my sacral chakra. I believe it was a purging of toxic waste that had been housed in my body and finally came to the place of release.

In chapter 6, "Spiritual Chronology, of Sorts," which addressed past-life regressions, I spoke of bodily abuse when I was pregnant as a black woman in a past life. This, I believe, was a purging of what my soul is releasing in this body.

My spiritual teacher messaged me, asking, "What's going on, Celeste?"

My answer: "My body is acting out what is going on in the external world."

We have been existing in the exhaustion of the third-dimensional world, consisting not only of COVID-19 but also of complete systemic upheaval and chaos. There is great fear among many who keep asking questions, for which there are no answers, which utters bleakness and despair. Those who recognize the shift are busily working in their assigned roles as light workers to help eradicate fear on a spiritual, physical, mental, and cellular level, while aiding the ushering in of the New Age.

My story is like many others that have been shrouded in sadness and devastation. In this writing, you have experienced but a few, as you either felt joy or experienced tears as you read through the pages. On my behalf, I would like to add the light!

As I send this memoir to publication, I will state once more that we live on planet earth school. There are many lessons to be learned here. There are many signs to guide us, but you must pay attention, or you will miss them. You are the warriors and the lovers. What you do does count. Even the smallest of thoughts manifest. Are you willing to be responsible for them? Are you willing to accept the consequences?

Consider *The Four Agreements* by Don Miguel Ruiz:

1. Speak impeccably. Speak your truth.
2. Don't take anything personally.
3. Don't make assumptions.
4. Do your best.

It is in practicing the laws of the universe that we find peace and freedom.

The eyes of the ancestors, the great masters, and all heavenly beings are upon us, waiting to guide us and bring us through this cataclysmic space-time journey that we are experiencing. Do not let fear be the tour guide; rather, know that the divine-source energy/God/all spirits of light and love are your constant companions.

Be the change that brings about the highest good for all humans and nature on this planet, for as we are all interconnected, the healing occurs. And so it is.

Lightworkers, shine your Lights.
Dance to the rhythm of the Soul.
If you are out of Beat, go within, connect
For in this space, Healing occurs.

After silence, that which comes nearest to expressing the inexpressible is music.
—Aldous Huxley

The Freedom Fighter/The Lover

Who is this woman who carries a sword in one hand?
Whose song is a heartfelt ballad,
A voice heard, thundering to the masses,
Whose longing is the greatest love story?
My sadness lies in battle, my joy in love.
A beautiful angel,
Armored for battle,
Lying among the soft grasses,
Marching into glory,
A Legion of one,
The heart of a Saint,
The Vision of Light,
Purging from darkness,
The Freedom Fighter/The Lover!

Printed in the United States
by Baker & Taylor Publisher Services